"Sun and McClellan compel us to remei ▮▮▮▮ campus conversations on First Amendmen., ...- M000102155
In every chapter, they prompt us to contemplate what socially just and 'inclusive freedom' could look like when students, faculty, and administrators partner to create a campus community that is both welcoming, inclusive and provides opportunities for robust freedom of expression."
—**Dr. Mary Jo Gonzales**, *Vice President for Student Affairs,*
Washington State University

"The authors resoundingly illuminate the tenuous balancing act required of campus leaders in addressing application of the First Amendment within higher education while supporting successful learning environments and thoughtful student experiences. Through seamless use of myriad examples, from court decisions to case studies, Sun and McClellan explicate the growing tension between freedom of expression, inclusion, and diversity of thought. Extending the conversation beyond curricular and co-curricular impacts, to include digital and community intersections, invites multiple leaders to engage in proactive planning and framework development to navigate campus clashes moving forward. This is a must read for new and seasoned leaders alike."
—**Dr. Brian O. Hemphill**, *President, Radford University*

"Issues related to free speech on college campuses may be one of the most important challenges we face as higher education leaders. Virtually every day, college campuses are at the nexus between free speech, hate speech, issues of equity and social justice, and harassment—often with no clear way forward. This book comes at a perfect time as these complex issues are being litigated and tested every day on the American college campus."
—**Dr. Kevin Kruger**, *President, NASPA*

"This remarkable book drives home the need for strong educational leadership at a time when divisive speech issues threaten the very blanket of free expression and association upon which institutions of higher learning depend. The law must inform critical leadership; but this is no time to simply defer to lawyers to fix things for us. This interdisciplinary book is pure educator's gold, a gift in a time of great need from authors with vast operational experience in higher education and sharp legal acuity."
—**Professor Peter Lake**, *Charles A. Dana Chair and*
Professor of Law, Stetson University

Student Clashes on Campus

This book unpacks the tension between free speech and the social justice priority to support all students. Drawing on court cases, institutional policies and procedures, and notable campus practices, this book answers the question: How do campus leaders develop interests of social justice and create a campus that is inclusive and inviting of all identities while also respecting students' free speech rights? This useful guide provides insights about the myriad of challenges that campus leaders have faced, along with practical approaches to address these issues on their own campuses. Experts Sun and McClellan interrogate the assumptions, thoughts, events, rules, and actions often at-play when free expression clashes with a college's mission of diversity, inclusion, and social justice. This book helpfully guides campus leaders to consider a series of legal frameworks and promising policies as solutions for balancing social justice and free speech.

Jeffrey C. Sun is Professor of Higher Education and Affiliate Professor of Law at the University of Louisville, USA.

George S. McClellan is Associate Professor of Higher Education at the University of Mississippi, USA.

Student Clashes on Campus

A Leadership Guide to Free Speech

Jeffrey C. Sun and
George S. McClellan

Routledge
Taylor & Francis Group

NEW YORK AND LONDON

First published 2020
by Routledge
52 Vanderbilt Avenue, New York, NY 10017

Simultaneously published in the UK
by Routledge
2 Park Square, Milton Park, Abingdon, Oxon OX14 4RN

Routledge is an imprint of the Taylor & Francis Group, an informa business

Library of Congress Cataloguing-in-Publication Data
A catalog record for this book has been requested

ISBN: 978-0-367-03073-5 (hbk)
ISBN: 978-0-367-03075-9 (pbk)
ISBN: 978-0-429-02021-6 (ebk)

Typeset in Sabon
by Apex CoVantage, LLC

Contents

Preface

Higher education in the United States has been loud and messy from its first days to its contemporary form. That should come as no surprise. Indeed, it should be taken as a sign of vigor and a hallmark of success. Would we as a nation really want something as important as higher education, which serves as a center for learning, research, and service to communities near and far, to be marked by quiet classrooms, hallways, and public spaces where only certain people are permitted to speak and only in certain ways? Students, staff, and faculty (along with a host of constituents) are engaging one another every day on college and university campuses. Their collective voices are sometimes harmonious and sometimes discordant, but there are always reasons to be excited about the potential of what might lie ahead and they serve as a call to be involved in shaping that future.

Students have been raising their voices on college campuses from the earliest days of American higher education, and college leaders have been seeking advice on how to handle such situations for just about the same length of time (Dickey, 2016). The ways in which student voices are put forward and are received have altered over time as the relationship between student and institution has shifted from *in loco parentis* to contractual client to co-creator. Of course, it is not just students who have spoken up and out. Faculty, and in some instances staff, have also expressed themselves broadly and with great fervor. Hofstadter (1970) traces issues of academic freedom and faculty speech back to Colonial times. As with developments in the relationship between student and institution, the changing nature of the professoriate, the emergence of the professional class, and shifts in the ways in the relationship between employer and employee have also given rise to evolving expectations with regard to employee speech. As higher education has evolved over time in the United States, matters of free speech have consistently presented themselves on the campuses of our nation's colleges and universities.

Similarly, while some may think of them as a more recent development, issues of inclusion have also been present from the founding days of our nation and its very first institutions of higher learning. Hurtado (2003) very carefully and thoughtfully lays out the ways in which the expansion of the United States drove changes in higher education and the ways in which those changes and the demographics of the population and of students interacted with one another over time.

Higher education values both free speech and inclusion as important in and of themselves and also as essential elements of successfully fulfilling its purposes. There is no doubt that there may be times when one can reasonably question the extent to which those values are merely espoused, but there is ample evidence that there are also times when institutions are truly trying to live them out as enacted. There are also times when these two values are not readily aligned. Moments when free speech (and other First Amendment freedoms) may, at least in some ways, appear to inhibit inclusivity on campus. Such conflicts can lead to court cases, hard feelings, loss of students, staff, or faculty, political problems, and other forms of diminished capacity of the individuals and the institution. Those same conflicts could also lead to better and more positive outcomes depending on the ways in which the campus community has prepared itself to work through the challenges and look for the opportunities. This book is about those moments, that preparation, and those choices.

We have several goals in presenting this book to readers. First, we hope to present information on contemporary law and policy in the area of free speech and inclusion. Second, we hope to share practical recommendations for practice. Third, we hope to offer broad frameworks beyond law and policy which can serve to augment decision-making in ways that are consistent with institutional mission.

Our audience for this book is as broad within higher education as the topic itself. Campus leaders, including senior academic and administrative officers, faculty, staff, and students, may find the information to be informative and helpful in their decision-making and campus governance roles. The book could also be a valuable resource for students and faculty in graduate higher education programs as they develop ideas on how to help assure the success of college students and the institutions which they serve. Finally, we imagine that those involved in the development of higher education policy at the system, state, or federal level might make use of the book to inform their efforts.

ASSUMPTIONS, AUTHORS' VOICES, AND ADVICE

We have tried to keep in mind the diversity of institutional contexts across the landscape of higher education as we have developed the content for this book. First Amendment freedoms are only an inherent concern at public institutions; similar rights may be extended as a matter of contract, policy, and practice or through local or state law at private institutions. That said, we have tended to use phrases like free speech or First Amendment freedoms for the sake of expediency throughout the chapters.

Similarly, matters of governance, nomenclature, and organization vary across individual institutions, systems of higher education, and types of institutions. We have tried to write in ways that are reflective and respectful of that rich variety, but it is possible that we may have overlooked an important nuance in particular settings. We regret any resulting lack of clarity in such instances.

We address staff and faculty speech and inclusion in the book, but a good deal of our discussion is focused on students on campus. This focus reflects a number of practical considerations. First, and we believe unfortunately, non-faculty college and university staff have fairly limited free speech rights. Second, contention surrounding faculty speech is often (though not always) centered on situations involving their interactions of one type or another with students. Third, as a matter of both sheer numbers and as a proportion of court cases, situations related to student speech and inclusion are far and away the more common circumstance—and often the most personally and politically fraught.

There are times in the book where we speak of the value of inclusion, and at other times we use the language of social justice. The two are not one and the same, and our choices throughout have been intentional. Not all campuses have adopted the language and principles of social justice. Neither have the courts in our country. As sorely tempted as we were to make the argument for change in this regard, our goals for this book led us in a different direction. That said, we cannot stress clearly or often enough that both higher education and the court systems are, in our view, like all the institutions in our country in reflecting systemic privilege and oppression born of our collective histories. This recognition is just one of the reasons that we argue throughout the book for looking beyond merely the legal framework in seeking to build campus communities where free speech and inclusion are not seen as inherently at odds and where, when tensions arise, they are understood in the context of a critical consciousness.

While we share broadly similar philosophies and perspectives, this book is written by two friends and colleagues with very different life and professional experiences. We have distinctive personal and academic voices which are evident in the chapters that follow. Our hope is that readers will find the variance to be refreshing rather than frustrating.

Finally, while we address contemporary law and policy matters throughout the book, nothing we have written is intended to serve as legal advice.

Providing that type of advice on a national level would be unwise and unhelpful given the way in which state and local laws also must be considered as a part of decision-making. Readers are encouraged to consult with their own counsel pertaining to particular matters at hand on their campuses.

DESCRIPTION OF THE DISCUSSION

Chapter 1 presents an overview of historical and contemporary developments with regard to free speech and inclusion on American college and university campuses. This chapter provides a set of introductory legal concepts and frameworks to analyze several tension points among student, staff, and faculty rights and responsibilities, on the one hand, and interests of equity and inclusion, on the other hand.

One way of understanding life on college campuses is to distinguish between the broad domains of the curriculum and co-curriculum, and we have organized Chapters 2 and 3 accordingly. Expressions and behaviors within the academic domain such as curricular matters, classroom interactions, and other learning environments including internships, field-placements, class projects, and study abroad are discussed in Chapter 2. Courts have historically granted colleges and universities fairly wide latitude when it comes to matters of the curriculum, though it is also an area in which students' speech is not without protection. Chapter 3 surveys a series of expressive activities, involving college students and potentially other campus community members, but these expressions are of the nature to be considered outside of the traditional academic domain.

Chapter 4 explores an area that has been less developed in the law, practice, and policies of postsecondary education—digital communication. Social media adds to the complexity to free speech situations because these expressions, which often include photos and words, have a greater distribution, easier access, and potential anonymity. This chapter reveals the dynamics of who has access, who may disseminate, and what may be replicated without penalty. It examines the power, influence, and roles and responsibilities of multiple actors in a situation.

While scholars in higher education presented the *Closing of the American Mind* (Bloom, 1987) and *Opening of the American Mind* (Levine, 1996) as competing positions to the conservative/liberal dialogue about higher education, other more powerful actors directed the narrative around free speech and campus dialogue in more forceful ways. Specifically, Chapter 5 uncovers the role of legislators at the federal and state levels along with their allies, who have influenced federal and state policies (though more significantly at the state level) by creating laws that penalize postsecondary institutions for restrictions, even when there are mission-oriented purposes.

Chapter 6 wraps up the book by posing suggestions for campus practices and policies of the future. It offers several frameworks for decision-making while drawing back to legal rules and professional practices discussed in earlier chapters. In doing so, this chapter presents ways to draw on the campus community for support and reminds readers to not lose sight of the ethical and professional standards, which extend beyond the law. We even entertain the idea that there are just some issues worth availing the institution to a threat of a lawsuit without breaching one's duties to the organization as a leader.

CONCLUSION

Both of us acknowledge that our identities as professionals who are highly socialized in the systems of the law and higher education and that the socialization processes have shaped our choice of this topic and our discussion of it. That said, we are hopeful that those identities situate us to offer advice born of our personal experiences as persons who have experienced both privilege and oppression. Those same identities have provided us with plentiful opportunities to consider matters of speech and inclusion both at the personal and professional level.

The degree to which we have succeeded in our goals and aspirations is up to our readers to determine. Please let us hear from you about your thoughts on our work and on the broader topics it addresses. Thank you.

REFERENCES

Bloom, A. (1987). *Closing of the American mind.* New York: Simon and Schuster.

Dickey, J. (2016, May 31). The revolution on America's campuses. *Time.* Retrieved from http://time.com/4347099/college-campus-protests/

Hofstadter, R. (1970). *Academic freedom in the age of the college.* New Brunswick, NJ: Transaction Publishers.

Hurtado, S. (2003). Institutional diversity in American higher education. In S. Komives & D. Woodard (Eds.), *Student services: A handbook for the profession* (4th ed., pp. 23–44). San Francisco: Jossey-Bass.

Levine, L. W. (1996). *The opening of the American mind.* Boston, MA: Beacon Press.

Acknowledgments

George S. McClellan is indebted to Jeffrey C. Sun for inviting him to be a part of this project and for his friendship and professional partnership and support since the day they met. Thanks as well to Rebecca Collazo and her colleagues at Routledge for their help in bringing this work forward. Hopefully there will be more opportunities to work together in the future.

George S. McClellan is grateful for the support of Dr. Neal Hutchens and his colleagues in Higher Education at the University of Mississippi. Their appreciation for the scholarship of practice, advice about transitioning to a full-time faculty role, and general good humor are invaluable. Thanks as well to Dean David Rock of the School of Education. He helps shape a community in which teaching, scholarship, and service are valued and where collegiality and professional engagement are the cherished norm.

George is particularly thankful for the students in Higher Education at the University of Mississippi. Their interest, enthusiasm, and commitment are inspiring, and learning with them is a true blessing. He also recognizes and celebrates all the students it has been his privilege to serve. As always, they are the best part of this work.

Finally, George wishes to acknowledge three people who have played a particularly important role in his understanding of the law in higher education and how it might be a part of making decisions in the best interests of college students and institutions of higher education. Tom Cline, former chief counsel for Northwestern University, provided an example of how a good relationship between administrator and attorney can be built and sustained. Peter Lake pointed to a way of focusing on the underlying principles of the law and the ways in which they connect with ethical principles and thoughtful andragogy in the curriculum and co-curriculum. Margaret J. Barr, friend and mentor, taught him law, leadership, laughter, and learning can all go together if we try. Thank you one and all.

George S. McClellan
Oxford, Mississippi

This work would not have been possible without an intellectually challenging and inspiring co-author, George S. McClellan. Jeffrey C. Sun has known George S. McClellan for over 15 years. During that time, George has served as a mentor and friend to Jeffrey teaching him about the roles and mission of higher education along with its stated and unstated policies and practices. He has also guided Jeffrey through the art of translation—translating legalese to comprehensible, consumable, and useful lessons into higher education practice.

Jeffrey C. Sun expresses his sincere gratitude to his students and colleagues, who regularly encourage him to put aside administrative tasks and re-engage in scholarship. It is has been a rejuvenating activity, which he hopes to continue for many more years. Jeffrey C. Sun is also appreciative to the team at Routledge—Rebecca and Heather, who have shepherded this publication with clear guidance and support.

Finally, nobody has been more important in the pursuit of this project than family members. Their encouragement, expressions of support, and love make scholarly writing even more rewarding and meaningful. Thank you—Jason, Ellen, Sylvester, Marina, mom, and dad.

Jeffrey C. Sun
Louisville, Kentucky

About the Authors

Jeffrey C. Sun is Professor of Higher Education, Affiliate Professor of Law, Department Chair, and Project Director & Principal Investigator for the U.S. Department of Education's Perkins funded project through the Kentucky Department of Education on Career & Technical Education, the U.S. Department of the Army's Master Educator Course (formerly Cadre & Faculty Development Course), the U.S. Department of Labor Veterans Accelerated Learning for Licensed Occupations with the Kentucky Science and Technology Center.

At Louisville, Dr. Sun established the university's first competency-based education program, obtained more than $11 million in federally sourced grants and contracts, advanced new initiatives for career and technical education teachers, established a partnership with the U.S. Army on cadre/faculty development and NCO leadership development, and led projects that expanded his department enrollments over 25% within three years. He also serves as a member of the "Forward50," which is a national thought-leadership group to advise Congress on the Higher Education Act.

Dr. Sun teaches and researches primarily in the areas of higher education law and policy. Dr. Sun's research examines the extent to which policy instruments or other legal actions (e.g., government mandates, judicial decisions, and legally binding, negotiated agreements) advance or inhibit the academic operations through college teaching, learning, and knowledge creation. This stream rests heavily on concepts of civil rights and civil liberties and has been published in venues such as *Cardoza Law Review*, *Education Law Reporter* (Westlaw), *Journal of College & University Law*, *Review of Higher Education*, *Teachers College Record*, and the *University of Pennsylvania's Journal of Constitutional Law*. In addition, Dr. Sun has four books: *Law and educational inequality: Removing barriers to educational opportunities* with Susan

Bon (2015); *Law, policy, and higher education: Cases and materials* with Gordon Gee, T.K. Daniel, and Patrick Pauken (2012); *Intellectual property in the information age* with Ben Baez (2009); and *Barriers to distance education: Governmental, legal, and institutional* with Arthur Levine (2003).

Dr. Sun taught previously at the University of North Dakota, Teachers College of Columbia University, and New York University. Also, while at Teachers College, he served as the Director of Academic Administration.

Today, Dr. Sun serves on the Executive Committee for the Association for the Study of Higher Education's Board of Directors and Chair of the Finance/Budget Committee. Dr. Sun received a BBA and an MBA from Loyola Marymount University, a law degree (J.D.) from the Moritz College of Law at The Ohio State University, and an M.Phil. and a Ph.D. from Columbia University.

George S. McClellan is Associate Professor of Higher Education at the University of Mississippi. Prior to joining the students and colleagues there, he served for ten years as the vice chancellor for student affairs at Indiana University—Purdue University Fort Wayne (IPFW). McClellan also held the position of vice president for student development at Dickinson State University in Dickinson, North Dakota, and has supported students in a variety of roles at the University of Arizona and Northwestern University.

He is the (co)author or (co)editor of numerous books, chapters, and articles on student affairs and higher education. His books and monographs include *A Good Job: Campus Employment as High Impact Practice* (2018) with K. Creager and M. Savoca; *Budgets and Financial Management in Higher Education* (2011 & 2018) with Margaret Barr; *The Handbook for Student Affairs Administration* with J. Stringer (2009 & 2016); *Making Change Happen in Student Affairs: Challenges and Strategies* with M. Barr and A. Sandeen (2014); *The Handbook for College Athletics and Recreation Administration* with C. King and D. Rockey, Jr. (2012); *Stepping Up and Stepping Out: Helping Students Transition to the Real World* with J. Parker (2012); *In Search of Safer Communities: Emerging Practices for Student Affairs in Addressing Campus Violence* with M. Jablonski, E. Zdziarksi, D. Ambler, R. Barnett-Terry, L. Cook, J. Dunkle, R. Gatti, E. Griego, and J. Kindle (New Directions in Student Services, 2008); *Gambling on Campus* with T. Hardy and J. Caswell (New Directions in Student Services, 2006); and *Serving Native American Students* with M. Fox and S. Lowe (New Directions in Student Services, 2005).

McClellan has served in a number leadership positions in student affairs professional associations. He was a member of the editorial board of both the *Journal of College Student Development* and the *Journal of College and Character*. He received the Outstanding Contribution to Research in American Indian Higher Education award from the Native American Network of the American College Personnel Association in 2002 and the Annuit Coeptis Senior Scholar Award from that association in 2017. McClellan served as a member of the National Association of Student Personnel Administrators (NASPA) Foundation Board, a founding member of that NASPA's Administrators in Graduate and Professional Student Services Community and its Indigenous Peoples Knowledge Community, and as chair or co-chair of that association's Task Force on Gambling and its Ad Hoc Work Group on the Voluntary System of Accountability. He was recognized by the NASPA Foundation as a Pillar of the Profession in 2010.

McClellan, a frequent presenter, speaker, and consultant on a variety of topics in student affairs and higher education, received his Ph.D. in Higher Education from the University of Arizona (2003). Both his M.S.Ed. in Higher Education (1998) and B.A. in English and American Literature (1982) were earned from Northwestern University.

Chapter One

Overview
The Clashing Interests, Rights, and Responsibilities

Mass protestors, smoke bombs, broken windows, flung objects into buildings, and uncontained fires . . . these collective events were sufficient for the University of California at Berkeley to cancel a public talk on February 1, 2017. The scheduled speaker, Milo Yiannopoulos, who, at the time, was the tech editor for Breitbart News, had planned to address attendees on the campus known for its historical position of stimulating open dialogue and debate about social and political issues, yet safety concerns precluded continuing the event. As the Berkeley Chancellor Nicholas Dirks (2017) wrote, "My administration reluctantly took that step [of cancelling the event] only after determining that both the speaker's and the public's safety was highly endangered."

Milo, as he is often referenced simply through his first name with little need to attach his surname, is a provocateur. He has been dubbed a "professional hatemonger" (Edge, 2017), a "conservative firebrand" (Bauer-Wolf, 2017), and "professional agitator" (Resnick & Collins, 2016). Referencing his college speaking circuit as the "Dangerous Faggot Tour," Milo, a politically conservative, gay white male, schedules or is invited by campus groups to speak on college campuses. He is often found "shouting to stop immigrants, feminists, political correctness, and any non-Western culture" (Stein, 2016). He addresses topics and presents claims that often ignite anger, resentment, outrage, and other emotions because his statements are perceived to demean, mischaracterize, and ostracize by spewing hate. Milo knows of his effect on audiences and other observers. In his self-proclaimed, vanity press book, he presents chapter titles with perceptions that others "hate" him for his views—for example, "Why the Progressive Left Hates Me," "Why the Alt-Right Hates Me," "Why Twitter Hates Me," "Why Feminists Hate Me," "Why the Media Hates Me," "Why Black Lives Matter Hates Me," "Why the Media Hates Me," Why Establishment Gays Hate Me," Why Establishment Republicans Hate Me," and "Why Muslims

1

Hate Me" (Yiannopoulos, 2017; see also, McClurg, 2017). Yiannopoulos has a following. He recognizes in the tenth chapter of his book that "Gamers Don't Hate Me" (Yiannopoulos, 2017). He also unabashedly touts "Why My College Tours Are So Awesome" (Yiannopoulos, 2017).

Milo, along with Steve Bannon, Ann Coulter, Charles Murray, Ben Shapiro, Richard Spencer, and others have challenged the boundaries of free speech on college campuses, often by provoking hecklers and other protestors.

Provocateurs are not new to college campuses, yet higher education institutions across the country have faced news headlines that have been unflattering evaluations of how campus leaders have addressed free speech, campus safety, diversity and inclusion, and community concerns. As the book traces, campus leaders have, perhaps unintentionally, limited college students' First Amendment rights by prescribing many hurdles, overreacting to possible fears, neglecting to draw on existing policies in a consistent manner, or failing to draw connections among events that would pose a different response when viewed in their entirety. In light of prior missteps by campus leaders, the authors present a series of frameworks and legal rules as well as promising policies and practices, which offer useful approaches or solutions when analyzed under the proper setting and applicable assumptions. To reach that goal, this book intends to guide campus leaders to consider these factors in a conversational, story-telling manner about the key areas to discuss when investigating how competing values in higher education potentially clash with the First Amendment.

One final word before moving forward with the discussion; while we offer information and analysis of legal matters and recommendations for policy and practice, nothing in this book is intended as legal advice. We encourage readers to consult with campus counsel and, while giving due deference to their professional opinions and suggestions, to keep in mind that advice and decisions are two different things.

FIRST AMENDMENT APPLICATIONS

The First Amendment permeates throughout these campus incidents. Campus leaders pause when protests, provocative events, and harmful messages are at issue because we have to ask ourselves, what are the college's principles and policies around free speech, and are we subject to the First Amendment of the U.S. Constitution?

Free speech policies are nowhere more important than a college, which fosters inquiry, challenges status quo, and serves as an incubator of ideas. Even a U.S. Supreme Court case opined that college professors and their students "must always remain free to inquire, to study and to evaluate, to gain new maturity and understanding; otherwise our civilization will stagnate and die" (Sweezy v. New Hampshire, 1957). With this social value on democratic idealism, it is not surprising that the First Amendment grants broad rights, and "state colleges and universities are not enclaves immune from the sweep" of this constitutional provision (Healy v. James, 1972, p. 180). Yet, research, case law, and practice suggest that college administrators do not easily interpret or apply correct nomenclature to First Amendment law, and even college administrators at private colleges inadvertently reference rights as governed by the First Amendment, when those rights do not apply because the legal relationship between a private college and its students is contractual in nature, not constitutionally based (Sun, Hutchens, & Sponsler, 2014). Placing the significance of the law in context, the fundamentals of the First Amendment's free speech provisions and cases offer insights on the potential clash between the First Amendment and the higher education values of diversity and inclusion.

Sources of Law

Our legal analysis begins with an understanding of who is covered by the First Amendment and other applicable laws. As the First Amendment has made clear, government actors, such as administrators, staff, and professors at public colleges, shall not make policies or take actions "prohibiting the free exercise thereof; or abridging the freedom of speech, . . . or the right of the people peaceably to assemble, and to petition the government for a redress of grievances" without violating individual rights (Delegates of the Constitutional Convention, 2005). These powers are broad for speakers and, in more recent times, have challenged the cultural minority rather than the cultural hegemony through events such as questioning feminism, raising support for European heritage, targeting racial equity efforts, and attacking sexual identities. As we will see, the First Amendment, when applicable, is powerful.

The First Amendment of the U.S. Constitution is not the only source of law which campus leaders wrestle with as they address college students' assertion of free speech rights. Another source of law that presents a quality and nature similar to the First Amendment, but originates at the state level, exists in several states. For instance, in California, the Leonard Law "prohibits private [colleges] with a nonsectarian (e.g., nonreligious) mission from making or enforcing any college policy that would lead to student disciplinary action solely for acts protected as free speech" (Hutchens & Sun, 2014, p. 3). Similarly, in New Jersey, the state constitution holds additional protections. As the case *State v. Schmid* (1980) articulated, "State constitutions may be distinct repositories of fundamental rights independent of the federal Constitution" (p. 628). A landmark decision examined whether a political advocate trespassed onto the private college campus in New Jersey and could be barred from distributing and selling political materials at Princeton University. The New Jersey Supreme Court observed that the private college may provide regulations limiting the speaker's rights, but it failed to sufficiently do so in this instance. Because the private college did not take steps to limit outsiders from exercising free speech, the state court held that the private college failed to articulate any "standards, aside from the requirement for invitation and permission, for governing the actual exercise of expressional freedom . . . nor did the regulations deal adequately with the time, place, or manner for individuals to exercise their rights of speech and assembly" (p. 632). Further, the alleged campus trespasser's use of the space fell within its normal or otherwise permissible use; the activity did not violate the private college's mission; and the political advocate was not disruptive to the private college's operations. Given these factors, the political advocate's expressions were permissible on the private college's campus and protected under the New Jersey Constitution. Thus, it is possible via state law to hold a private university to free speech rights of members from off campus. It is worth noting that following this case, Princeton University changed its policies about off-campus community members gaining access to its campus, so although the case informs us of potential free speech consequences for private colleges, it no longer applies to Princeton.

Free speech rights are not simply formal state laws that cover free speech or open access to public accommodations as discussed above. Free speech rights may also be granted through policies and practices, which are protected under state contract law. Colleges, particularly private colleges, may create policies and practices making them subject to state contract laws that include provisions which are similar to free speech requirements. For instance, according to Carnegie Mellon University, a private nonsectarian university, its policy creates a contractual relationship with its campus community stating:

> On Carnegie Mellon's campus, anyone [in the campus community] may distribute printed material, offer petitions for signature, make speeches, and hold protests or demonstrations outside university buildings. All such activities must be peaceful, avoiding acts or credible threats of violence and preserving the normal operation of the university. No event shall infringe upon the rights or privileges of anyone not in sympathy with it, and no one will be permitted to harm others, damage or deface property, block access to university

buildings or disrupt classes. The enforcement of these conditions will not depend in any way on the message or sponsorship of the act or event.

This policy provides a wide range of expressions, which are granted through contractual rights making the private college subject to its own rules.

In sum, the First Amendment only applies, generally speaking, to public colleges and actions arising from employees at the public institution. The First Amendment as a constitutional matter is critical to the discussion in this book, so public colleges have the most at stake. Yet, other laws, such as state constitutions, state laws over free speech (e.g., California's Leonard Law), and contract law via college policies, may hold private colleges to the same or similar standards of practice as the First Amendment. Because the focus of the national challenges has rested largely on the First Amendment, which affords constitutional protections for citizens to speak freely without government infringement, we place primary emphasis on our analysis to public colleges as governmental entities. Free speech at private colleges typically maintains limited rights, relative to public universities. Nonetheless, in some instances, private colleges have adopted First Amendment principles, at least in part, or referenced these principles as important values. In such situations, those policies are subject to contract law or other state sources of law, not the First Amendment (Daniel, Gee, Sun, & Pauken, 2012).

Types of Speech

Court cases on free speech consistently deconstruct the expression at issue to determine if the type of speech qualifies for protections under the law. The First Amendment requires a careful examination of whether an expression constitutes "free speech" that is protected by the First Amendment (Daniel, Gee, Sun, & Pauken, 2012). As a default rule, courts have ruled that political, social, scientific, artistic, and religious expressions are typically protected akin to having a special legal shield because they represent the kind of speech that the law clearly intended to protect (Sun, Hutchens, & Sponsler, 2014).

The question, then, becomes whether the expression at issue falls within those protected categories. For instance, in a political speech scenario, a student newspaper at a public college published an image depicting policemen raping the Statue of Liberty and the Goddess of Justice (Papish v. Board of Curators, 1973). Underneath the cartoon, the message read, "With Liberty and Justice for All." That same newspaper issue included an article entitled

"Mother f— Acquitted," recounting a trial of a New York City teenager who was a member of an organization known as "Up Against the Wall, Mother f—" and was acquitted on an assault charge. The public college expelled the student journalist for violating "generally accepted standards of conduct" and asserted that she violated the policy on "indecent conduct or speech" (Papish v. Board of Curators, 1973, p. 668). The U.S. Supreme Court disagreed, and the Justices concluded that the cartoon and article were not constitutionally obscene, but instead, the expressions were con- stitutionally protected as political speech because the message was a matter of public concern. To overcome the special protections, the public college would be required to show a compelling state interest with clear goals and that such regulatory policy was narrowly tailored by implementing the least restrictive means to achieve those goals. That demonstration was not adequately presented, so the public college lost the case.

This case signaled to the legal community that the First Amendment has significant leeway. As Bob Woodward and Scott Armstrong (1979) recounted, Justice Powell, who wrote the primary decision for this case, "was sufficiently sensitive to the language that in place of the word 'Fucker,' he used 'F—.' But he expressed no doubt that this was political speech under the First Amendment." Thus, while a campus administrative team is likely to consider weighing interests such as free speech and potentially obscene communication. The default rule suggests examining whether the expres- sion has redeeming value, such as political speech, as a means to overcome assertions of an obscene communication. This approach is critical to analyz- ing expressions that thread thinly between potential protected speech under the First Amendment and perceived harmful speech that touches on matters of diversity and inclusion, which may also shape the campus climate.

Also, although the focus so far has been on verbal and written communi- cation as illustrations of free speech claims, the court cases have protected other forms in which free speech protections are applicable. Specifically, courts have held that certain forms of expression are legally classified as an inherently expressive activity for which the law values. These expressions include symbolic communication, which could be wearing an armband to protest a war (Tinker v. Des Moines, 1969), burning a flag to demon- strate opposition to national policy (Texas v. Johnson, 1989), and wearing empty holsters to advocate for gun rights (Smith v. Tarrant County College District, 2010). As a whole, many expressions likely qualify as permis- sible expressions under the First Amendment, and this special protection over political, social, scientific, artistic, and religious expressions presents challenges to a college's diversity and inclusion priority because the law protects potentially offensive expressions that could negatively harm an organizational climate when it is unable to curb such expressions.

Behaviors v. Speech

The line between permissible, protected speech and inappropriate behavior is a difficult one for campus leaders and the courts. When discussing types of speech, the courts have referenced, though sometimes inferentially, instances when the expression crosses the line to prohibited conduct, which is not protected under the First Amendment, or the speech presents lower levels of protection. Expressions that contain harassing messages are a form of expression that may arise to prohibited conduct. One public college properly explains to its campus community when actions arise to harassment and is prohibited conduct. Its policy states:

> Actions constitute harassment, if they substantially interfere with another's educational or employment opportunities, peaceful enjoyment of residence, physical security, and they are taken with a general intent to engage in the actions and with the knowledge that the actions are likely to substantially interfere with a protected interest identified in the subsection above.
>
> (Arizona State University, 2019)

The policy is very detailed to conform to the law. Harassment as a prohibited conduct includes a demonstration that the act "substantially interfere[s] with another's educational or employment opportunities, peaceful enjoyment of residence, [or] physical security." That behavior is also "taken with a general intent" based on a reasonable person's perspective "to engage in the actions" and the person acting in such manner has "knowledge" or an awareness "that the actions are likely to substantially interfere with a protected interest identified." In other words, harassment is a layered showing of the effect, reasonable belief of the intent, and knowledge of the actions. Of course, the analysis is preceded with the inquiry of whether the expression was political, social, scientific, artistic, or religious in nature. If no, then the inquiry would consist of whether the expression crossed the line into prohibited conduct such as harassment as outlined above.

Harassment is one of numerous actions that may overcome an assertion of free speech. The courts have identified the following categories of expressions that cross into other impermissible behaviors:

- obscenity, which amounts to an expression that an average community member considers as appealing to prurient interest, is classified as patently offensive, and lacks social, political, and scientific value;
- "true" threats, which occurs when a speaker communicates a serious expression of intent to commit an act of unlawful violence to a particular individual or a clearly identifiable group of individuals;

- defamation, which reflects false and defamatory expressions about another without any privilege to make such expressions;
- disruptive expressions, which are associated with conduct that actually or is reasonably forecasted to lead to material disruption or substantial disorder, but must be more than mere offensive speech such as hecklers who prevent featured speakers from addressing an audience; and
- harassment, which is unwelcome and objectively sufficiently severe, pervasive, or persistent experiences (e.g., harassment based on sex, race, national origin) creating a hostile environment that interferes with or limits the ability of the education program such as learning.

For instance, what may initially be classified as expressions may lead to acts of sexual harassment. In a case involving a college couple who broke up, the ex-boyfriend tweeted several disparaging messages such as "Oh right, negative boob job. I remember her," "If I could say one thing to you it would probably be 'Go fuck yourself you piece of shit.' #butseriouslygofuckyourself #crazyassex," and "Lol, she goes up to my friends and hugs them and then unfriends them on Facebook. #psycho #lolwhat." The tweets by themselves, unless they were extraordinary and arising to objectively sufficiently severe, pervasive, or persistent experiences and impeded a student's right to learn or participate in an education program, would likely be protected under First Amendment free speech for a public college setting. However, when placed in context, these tweets reflected a larger behavioral concern. Specifically, preceding the tweets was a criminally driven no contact order placed on the ex-boyfriend when he

> physically restrained [his ex-girlfriend], took her phone from her, threatened to commit suicide if she broke up with him, threatened to spread rumors about her, and threatened to make the University of Kansas's "campus environment so hostile, [that she] would not attend any university in the state of Kansas."
> (Yeasin v. Durham, 2018, p. 847)

These events violate the no contact order and present a hostile environment sexual harassment situation, which is not protected by the First Amendment.

A true threat, which is described above, also arises into impermissible conduct, not a protected expression. A case outside of the higher education context illustrates settings that could resemble a college context of true threats (State v. Taupier, 2018). In that case, the person claiming free speech rights had a court hearing challenging custody of his children.

Following the hearing, he wrote to several individuals about the judge presiding over his custody determination in which he stated: "(1) They can steal my kids from my cold dead bleeding cordite filled fists . . . as my [sixty] round [magazine] falls to the floor and [I'm] dying as I change out to the next [thirty rounds]"; (2) "[Bo]zzuto lives in [W]atertown with her boys and [n]anny . . . there [are] 245 [yards] between her master bedroom and a cemetery that provides cover and concealment"; and (3) "a [.308 caliber rifle] at 250 [yards] with a double pane drops [one-half inch] per foot beyond the glass and loses [7%] of [foot pounds] of force [at] 250 [yards]—nonarmor piercing ball ammunition" (State v. Taupier, 2018, pp. 156–157). The comments were not of a political, social, scientific, artistic, or religious expression. Instead, the directness of the message to the hearing officer along with specific information that communicates a serious expression of intent to commit an act of unlawful violence elevates words into prohibited conduct.

The words that may appear threatening require some analysis to determine if, indeed, they arise to prohibited conduct. A case involving public safety illustrates this level of inquiry when the court examined whether a true threat existed overcoming protections under the First Amendment. In that case, a police officer received complaints about comments on a van that frightened individuals in the community. The comments are not summarily treated as true threats when an individual reports concerns. The words and messaging need to be examined. The van had phrases such as "I AM A FUCKING SUICIDE BOMBER COMMUNIST TERRORIST!" as painted block letters on the back of the van (Fogel v. Collins, 2004, p. 827). The rear window had the message "PULL ME OVER! PLEASE, I DARE YA" (p. 827). Below the window in slightly smaller letters, the printed message stated: "ALLAH PRAISE THE PATRIOT ACT. . . . FUCKING *JIHAD* ON THE FIRST AMENDMENT! P.S. W.O.M.D. ON BOARD!" (p. 827). Among the collage of messages, a small American flag was pasted below the messages. Also, the "rest of the van was decorated with slogans and paintings that had no political or threatening character" (p. 827). This incident could foreseeably take place on a college campus and involve a public safety officer at a state college.

Because the incident was based on governmental actors (i.e., local law enforcement), the three panel judges on the federal court drew on the First Amendment. The federal appellate court ruled that the messages represented satirical or hyperbolic political speech, which is protected. In the court's analysis, the judges concluded that a reasonable person would not interpret the messages as a true threat of serious harm, and the van owner had no intentions to threaten serious harm to anyone. Thus, the message was protected under the First Amendment.

Although these exceptions to free speech offer some protections from harmful and offensive language, the courts have quite consistently ruled that these legal limits are circumscribed to avoid limiting expressions and furthering the aims of the First Amendment, which for public colleges include maintaining environments that serve as a marketplace of ideas (Bloucher, 2008). Further, there is no *per se* ban or limitation on inflammatory, insensitive, offensive, or hate speech.[1] The law has no special protections that fall within these specific categories, which again presents challenges to public colleges with equity and social justice values.

Forums and Spaces

So far, we have discussed the sources of law and how the type of speech or prohibited behaviors shape free speech law. The forum or the space and setting in which one presents a message or expression is another level of analysis with free speech cases. The First Amendment requires an analysis to categorize the forum or space in which the speech takes place. As a default, the First Amendment grants wide latitude to the speaker when the expressions are in settings that are considered a public forum (Sun, Hutchens, & Sponsler, 2014). Typically, spaces that are classified as a public forum are government property and places, which are not privately owned but accessible to the public. These spaces include streets, parks, sidewalks, and town squares.

Similarly, when a public college designates a space as a public forum, either by explicit declaration or its usage pattern, such as an identified free speech zone or open campus spaces that have regularly permitted protests or messaging, these spaces are considered designated public forums subject to traditional free speech regulations. As the court cases indicate, public colleges cannot prevent or limit speakers in these settings based on the content of the expression absent a compelling reason and the approach selected to limit that speech must be narrowly tailored to address that reason. The only limitations, by default, that may be asserted are reasonable restrictions based on time, place, and manner. For instance, the public college may restrict free speech to 9:00 am to 9:00 pm and limit amplification so as not to disrupt the library or academic buildings.

The standards to regulate someone's speech in these settings are very limited, but for the most part, the public college dictates whether it avails that forum as subject to these rules. If so, a speaker could convey rather hurtful messages with little recourse to stop the message. For instance, a student group may have reserved space in a quad to host an affirmative action bake sale. The pricing of the baked goods is then based significantly on the purchaser, not the baked item, with higher rates for individuals whom the group perceives as having more difficult admissions odds under a race conscious admission policy. This instance has happened on numerous campuses where, for example, black, Hispanic, and American Indian women paid 50 cents for a cupcake, white women paid $1, and white men paid $2. While the message would be considered offensive to many, the First Amendment protects such political expressions in forums considered a public forum or a designated public forum. Likewise, a student group may counter that message with a White Privilege bake sale. It may reverse the prices based on privilege status giving lower rates for the baked goods to white men, followed by white women, and so forth. In essence, the richness of the exchange and debate has not been lost.

A public college has more options as to how open it wishes to make its campus. If it chooses to do so and acts in a consistent manner, it could limit its spaces and control its campus access more (Sun, Hutchens, & Sponsler, 2014). The law permits public colleges to restrict spaces or other forums to certain classes of speakers (e.g., only students or only university employees) or certain classes of subjects (e.g., only for academic performances or only for theatrical productions) (Sun & Hutchens, 2014). These spaces are deemed limited public forums, and public colleges may place restrictions on the expressions so long as the policies are viewpoint neutral and reasonable in light of the purpose of the forum. Spaces that fall under a limited public forum could be an auditorium, recital hall, online community site for students, dining facility, student lounges for certain majors, bulletin board, and even an open grassy area within an enclosed campus.

Another location that is frequently referenced in First Amendment cases and a target for media criticisms is the academic setting, which is presented in greater detail in Chapter 2 of this book. These settings include a classroom, discussion board for online courses, internship/practicum experience, and labs (Sun, Hutchens, & Breslin, 2013). The courts have uniformly held these spaces as not a forum in which students at public colleges have a right to free speech except for symbolic speech that does not present a substantial or material disruption to the learning environment (e.g., wearing an empty holster to communicate a political statement about gun control). When it comes to the academic setting, particularly the classroom, public colleges have a right to regulate expressions in this environment with policies that are reasonably related to legitimate pedagogical concerns and are viewpoint neutral (Hazelwood v. Kuhlmeier, 1988; Sun, Hutchens, & Breslin, 2013). In other words, when the academic setting is at issue, policies may not curb political or ideological positions unless the limitations are based on some reasonable, learning-based justification, which may include professional standards of the field, but otherwise, public colleges have a great deal of latitude to limit students' expressions and provide a safe learning environment that permissibly advances diversity and inclusion values as a core tenet to learning (Hutchens, Sun, Blanchard, & Breslin, 2014).

It is important to note that while the forum in which expressions take place is critical to the analysis, not all spaces categorized within the forum analysis are physical locations such as free speech zones, parks, or auditoriums. A forum for expressions may include "space" on a bulletin board, website, student organization portal, funding for registered student organizations, and access to the use of the university trademark. For instance, if a public college permits registered student organizations to use its trademark, the college cannot later restrict other student groups it does not support such as a student association that advocates for marijuana law reforms or a newly registered group that advances Blue Lives Matter. Such action would arise to discrimination based on the content or viewpoint of the speech, and that action would violate the First Amendment (Gerlich v. Leath, 2017).

PHILOSOPHICAL AND OPERATIONAL DIFFERENCES

First Amendment principles are, at times, truly in conflict with college diversity and inclusion principles. The aims of these principles are simply different.

By some scholarly accounts, the intent of the First Amendment was envisioned to protect the nation from overbearing restrictions that precluded voices about governance and approaches to self-governance (Meiklejohn, 1965). Yet, the concept of political speech as a protection from government regulation is, in fact, much more expansive. A U.S. Supreme Court case highlighted the coverage of the law stating: "But our cases have never suggested that expression about philosophical, social, artistic, economic, literary, or ethical matters to take a nonexhaustive list of labels is not entitled to full First Amendment protection" (Abood v. Detroit Bd. of Educ., 1977, p. 231).[2] Despite the seemingly expanded coverage, philosophies of free speech law lead to operational differences and clear oppositional camps that have emerged as the law's effects on persons and communities have become more apparent.

Utilitarian Perspective

One interpretation of the First Amendment draws on a utilitarian perspective as captured by John Milton and John Stuart Mills. Milton subscribed to a truth-seeking approach that arises from a divine source, and it is theological and religiously based (Slagle, 2009). In John Milton's *Areopagitica*, he made clear that the search for truth through open debate and the competition of ideas presented an effective means for citizens to interrogate philosophies, theories, and ideas, which would lead to discerning the truth and rejecting falsehoods. Milton (1987) framed the inquiry as follows:

> And though all the winds of doctrine were let loose to play on the earth, so Truth be in the field, we do injuriously by licensing and prohibiting misdoubt her strength. Let her and Falsehood grapple; who ever knew Truth put to the worse in a free and open encounter?
> (p. 50)

Not surprisingly, his position, which largely explains the perspective followed for the First Amendment, offers a stance with the truism: "Give me the liberty to know, to utter, and to argue freely according to conscience, above all liberties" (Milton, 1987). This perspective draws on the agnostic view of words and ideas as efforts toward finding truth and discernment of policymaking and citizen determinations.

Of course, the law is not as straightforward, and as explained above, some exceptions exist—primarily to reduce protections on expressions that arise to prohibited conduct. In other words, the law has not fully adopted the Milton doctrinal stance that all expressions may hold equal weight. Adopting a perspective closely aligned with John Stuart Mills, the First Amendment law places some qualifiers to expressions. While Mills argued that "there ought to exist the fullest liberty of professing and discussing, as a matter of ethical conviction, any doctrine, however immoral it may be considered" (1978, p. 15), he did not intend a limitless approach to free expression. There were circumscribed views to free speech. In Mills's words, "The only purpose for which power can be rightfully exercised over any member of a civilized community, against his will, is to prevent harm to others" (p. 15). This perspective acknowledges the harm from true threats, defamation, and hostile environment harassment. Nonetheless, the free speech law and the philosophical position from which it derives still present coverage gaps when colleges seek different responses to advancing the diversity and inclusion goals.

When campuses frame their interest as placing diversity and inclusion as a threaded principle among their policies and practices, the utilitarian approach presents limited assistance. For instance, adopting the utilitarian approach, Papandrea (2017) argues that the "authority of public universities to restrict student speech is, or at least should be, quite narrow" (p. 1803). Affirming free speech principles, she cites examples of instances when campuses have too quickly punished students' expressions for offensive speech such as a Kansas State University student expelled for her

Snapchat picture "using cosmetic clay mask with the racially offensive caption, '[f]eels good to finally be a [racial slur]'" (Papandrea, 2017, p. 1805). Similarly, Bennett (2016) asserts that selected empirical evidence dispels the argument between speech, which is deemed as hate or offensive, and social harms. Further, he argues that hate speech regulation would present greater social harms by "empower[ing] lawmakers to barter away the right to free speech" when they are charged with determining which utterances would be protected and which would be prohibited" (Bennett, 2016, p. 522).

Critical Perspective

Although the utilitarian perspective serves as the general approach to First Amendment law, legal scholars and social scientists have noted the unintended effects of the law's philosophical foundations (Byrne, 1990; Delgado & Stefancic, 2017; Gordon & Johnson, 2003; Herbeck, 2018; Post, 1991; Turner, 1995). The law marginalizes groups of people, important values, and prevalent perspectives. Further, the effects include social and psychological harm (Delgado & Stefancic, 2017; Gordon & Johnson, 2003). Delgado and Stefancic (2017), who are legal scholars analyzing the effects of First Amendment on college campuses using a critical perspective, identified fundamental problems with the utilitarian approach as the basis to apply current legal principles to college campuses. They question the elitist approach to intellectual inquiry, and they recognize many instances in which the law disregards social issues that are in place now as a consequence of the past. Further, they recognize how the law fails to address the skewed distribution of communicative power such as social media messaging and other messaging tools advocating for hate and further marginalization. Finally, they also raise concerns about how the law fails to account for the nonphysical harms including significant psychological effects from speech that is currently protected under the law.

Even though colleges have a different mission and societal role, the traditional legal analyses constrain campus leaders from exercising protections they may like to apply (Byrne, 1990; Delgado & Stefancic, 2017). Accordingly, legal philosopher Stanley Fish questions the utilitarian approach asserting the flaw that "the consequences have been discounted in relation to a good that is judged to outweigh them" (Fish, 1994, p. 106).

Utilitarian Perspective as the Default

There may not be an easy answer to this legal debate. Keck (2016) posits that hate speech protections, if available, would create a double standard, "namely that legislative bans on hate speech communicate a message of exclusion to members of vulnerable groups who are left outside the scope of the bans' protection" (p. 100). That is, the effect of such bans would further messaging of marginalization by signaling unequal protections and citizenship unless uniformly applied, which presents a whole new set of legal complications. Accordingly, while there are still downsides to the U.S. First Amendment law, its simplified, line-drawing approach may be better than the alternatives presented in the literature and currently practiced in various European countries. It begets the question: How tightly should the law serve to restrict or support expressions on college campuses? Constitutional law scholar Robert Post rationalized the philosophical approach used to interpret First Amendment law by interrogating our deliberative self-determination as citizens. He wrote:

> [E]ither we decide to retain the ideal of democracy as deliberative self-determination and work to minimize the debilitating consequences of these criticisms, or we decide that these criticisms have so undermined the idea of deliberative self-determination that it must be abandoned and a different value for democracy embraced.
>
> (p. 327)

Around this time, other dialogue about the application of the First Amendment to public colleges facing the diversity and inclusion concern emerged searching for an alternative analysis. Several legal scholars have suggested special carve-outs for educational settings (see, e.g., Byrne, 1990; Delgado & Stefancic, 2017; Post, 1991). Indeed, college is a place to learn without abusive and targeted interferences that drive hate, humiliation, and forms of harassment. Yet, this approach of creating a different set of rules for educational settings has been countered with less fanfare through opposing legal scholarship and concerns about "coddling of the American mind" (Lukianoff & Haidt, 2015). Instead, a significant and long line of research agrees with the courts' application of First Amendment rules and principles to public colleges as with most government settings. In other words, rulings from the courthouses to the public parks inform and shape how public colleges operate when the issue is a matter of free speech.

At the end, this approach and others toward granting public colleges more autonomy to construct protections for arguably harmful or offensive and hateful expressions never seemed to generate any legal gravitational pull. Instead, First Amendment rulings continued to be announced, and their holdings continued to apply to public higher education—just as free speech cases held application to other governmental agencies including the department of motor vehicles, municipal parks, state environmental protection agencies, and regional airports.

WHAT'S AT STAKE?

The law does not extend as far as a famous quote often attributable to Voltaire. Declaring his position on free speech, he wrote: "I disapprove of what you say, but I will defend to the death your *right* to say it" (Tallentyre, 2003, p. 199). The message, while desirable in most settings of democracy, presents a difficult challenge for campus leaders to address. It highlights the colliding interests between the First Amendment and the diversity and inclusion mission for most of our campuses.

The stakes are high at a public college. If a campus administrator is at a public college and the issue is a First Amendment challenge, the law is not so forgiving. Constitutional errors that improperly infringe on the rights of students when the college administrator, who took such action, should have reasonably known that the action violated a student's constitutional rights, may face more than an institutional liability claim under the constitution. The student, whose constitutional rights were infringed, may assert a viable personal liability claim against the campus leaders. For instance, in *Husain v. Springer* (2007), a federal appellate court concluded that there were serious questions about whether a public college president was eligible for qualified immunity, which would have shielded her personally from the lawsuit. In that case, the college president nullified the student government elections and scheduled a new one because the student newspaper publicly supported a slate of candidates. The president responded in this manner because she wanted a fair election, and the student newspaper may have tainted that process. Nonetheless, the court ruled that the college president's actions violated the First Amendment of editors for the student newspaper. According to the court, she limited the students' viewpoints to express whom they believed would perform well on behalf of the student body. Also, the court concluded that the college president's actions had a chilling effect, when the newspaper staff felt compelled to scale back the elections coverage and avoid any candidate endorsements, for fear of another election nullification. With the effect of controlling students' voices, the federal appellate court requested a re-examination of the case to determine whether the public college president was eligible for qualified immunity in light of her actions. The court noted that the president of the public college should have known that her actions likely violated students' constitutional rights making her potentially subject to the lawsuit as an individual.

Similarly, discussing another case, *Orin v. Barclay* (2001), Daniel, Gee, Sun, and Pauken (2012) highlight the review of a qualified immunity claim for an interim dean of students and a campus security officer. One of these campus employees allegedly directed a campus preacher from speaking on overtly religious matters. If found to be true, such a restriction would have placed an impermissible discriminatory action based on the speaker's viewpoint. Because the preacher was otherwise permitted to use the campus space, public colleges may not curb one's rights based on the content or viewpoint without a compelling governmental interest, and if it does, the option must be narrowly tailored to meet that government interest. That notwithstanding, Daniel, Gee, Sun, and Pauken (2012) emphasize that the underlying concern in this case is that a "reasonable public official should have known that permitting [a preacher] to express his views on abortion only so long as those views were not religious in nature violated his First Amendment rights" and such error potentially drops the protections under qualified immunity (p. 562). Put simply, these cases are not simply about the financial recovery from damages and court fees, which the party suing seeks to capture. Yet, in such instances, campus leaders may be subject to personal liability for constitutional errors. Thus, the stakes are also high for individual administrators who act inappropriately when they should have known as a campus leader that their actions would violate a person's constitutional rights.

WHAT HAS CHANGED?

Diversity and inclusion are not new priorities for higher education. Court cases over the past 40 years demonstrate challenges to college access and social justice movements such as race conscious admissions practices (Regents of the University of California v. Bakke, 1978; Gratz v. Bollinger, 2003, 2003; Fisher v. University of Texas, 2013), diversity as a factor for financial aid support (Podberesky v. Kirwin, 1994), equal opportunity for program funding (Rosenberger v. Rector and Visitors of University of Virginia, 1995; Board of Regents of University of Wisconsin System v. Southworth, 2000), and inclusive membership for registered student organizations (Christian Legal Soc. v. Martinez, 2010).

Similarly, racial tensions and desires for action have also remained concerns. Drawing on late 1980 data from UCLA's Cooperative Institutional Research Program, one in four students who were surveyed reported racial conflicts on campus (Hurtado, 1992). According to a study published in the mid-1990s, more than half of surveyed faculty supported restrictions on racist and sexist expressions (Dey & Hurtado, 1996). Further, the Southern Poverty Law Center reported in the year 2000 that hate crimes and hurtful activities motivated by race, ethnicity, religion, and sexual orientation had increased over the prior period in which the data were tracked. The Anti-Defamation League (2018) also reported a 77% increase in white supremacist propaganda on college campuses between the 2016–2017 and 2017–2018.

Prior initiatives, cases, and reports present a few illustrations of longstanding concerns about diversity and inclusion on college campuses, and they demonstrate past efforts to advance a diversity and inclusion priority. Nonetheless, the progress seems to be minimal or possibly showing negative gains from the intended goals. Yet, protests and activism did exist back then as it does today. The difference is that those efforts seem relatively tame compared to recent news reports. Also, the evidence suggests changes in terms of the activism from inside and outside of higher education (Barnhardt, 2004; Dilley, 2019; Rhoads, 1998, 2016). Campus capacity to address the situations, which have played a role in stirring up the campus environment, have escalated and brought greater tensions between free speech, on the one hand, and diversity and inclusion, on the other. Notably, the differences between now and in the past are manifested through five distinct changes from the past several decades of campus free speech challenges.

Coordinated Speakers and Groups

One of the changes is the coordinated presence of provocative and antagonistic speakers and groups. Campuses have historically witnessed student movements, which were generated from oppositional perspectives with some coordination (Barnhardt, 2014). However, the coordination is even better today with groups such as Alt-right, Identity Evropa, Oath Keepers, Patriot Front, Rise Above Movement, and Turning Point. Also, there are a slew of speakers such as Milo Yiannopoulos, Ann Coulter, and Richard Spencer, who execute with a coordinated effort unlike the past campus protests. Further, counter-protesters have also formed coalitions and noteworthy rallies, such as Black Lives Matter, United Against Hate, and Antifa, and these events and groups have presented conflicting positions within our college campuses. Put simply, the coordinated efforts from provocateurs, protestors, and other expressive camps have changed the environment around campus climate and safety.

The data also illustrate the tensions on campus that lead to harmful expressions. The Clery Act (2019) disclosures, the number of hate crimes, which under the reporting regulations are offenses motivated by biases of race, national origin, ethnicity, religion, sexual orientation, gender, or disability, on college campuses or the defined immediate physical area, increased by 25% when comparing 2015 to 2016 reports (U.S. Department of Education, 2019). The increase is even more noticeable when you compare 2011 to 2016, which realized a nearly 40% increase. There may be some signs of reprieve. The numbers of hate crimes under Clery reporting guidelines dropped by nearly 13% from 2016 to 2017, but still the 2017 number of incidents was nearly 22% higher than 2011. Thus, hope for progress is relative to the recent past, and the data suggest changes from the past, which accounts for a heightened concern on our campuses.

The data also demonstrate significant activity through physical campus postings—even during this electronic, social media age. Between March 2016 and October 2017, the Southern Poverty Law Center (2017) identified 329 flyer incidents that reflected hate group messaging on 241 different campuses in the U.S. These messages included racist, Islamophobic, xenophobic, anti-immigration, and white nationalist messaging. In addition, some of the flyers included white propaganda and recruitment efforts expressing how "Our Future Belongs To Us" and "Our Destiny Is Ours" (Southern Poverty Law Center, 2017). These messages suggest that a slowing down on hate crimes on campus may not last long as efforts continue to spread anti-inclusionary slogans and gain more members with these shared values (Bauman, 2018; Moore & Bell, 2017).

College Students' Values

Generally speaking, college students' values have changed, and that perspective may be escalating the colliding rights between free speech and a diverse and inclusive campus environment. In a 2018 report, based on a Gallup and Knight Foundation survey, a representative sample of college students expressed interest in supporting both free speech rights and a diverse and inclusive society. Specifically, a majority of college students who responded indicated that protecting free speech rights (56%) and promoting a diverse and inclusive society (52%) are both extremely important aspects to our democratic society. However, when asked if the diversity and inclusion priority or free speech rights is more important, college students participating in the study placed the diversity and inclusion priority slightly higher than free speech rights, 53% to 46%, respectively. The survey results also reported a decline by 8% between 2016 and 2017 of students who would prefer an open campus environment that even allows for offensive speech. The data suggest that a shift in mindset and priorities for college students has taken place. These perspectives have not been well received by right-wing advocates. Notably, critics of college students' inclusionary and accepting perspectives have casted college students as overly sensitive, crybabies, libtards, social justice warriors, betas, and snowflakes. Blaming the liberal views on college campuses, former U.S. Attorney General Jeff Sessions characterized the development of college students as operating in non-inclusive environments that cater to students who are part of a "generation of sanctimonious, sensitive, supercilious snowflakes" (Quintana, 2018).

College students' perspectives shape campus activities. Student activism through expressions and behaviors have challenged and supported equity and social justice policies and priorities on college campuses. As the media have captured, many campuses have had to contend with disruptive hecklers seeking to silence speakers at campus engagements (Adams, 2017); demonstrations for and against campus monuments and building names that have historical associations with slavery and white supremacy (Arriaga, 2017; Patel, 2018); violent protests in response to controversial speakers, who espouse hateful messages (McMurtrie, 2017); and social media messages with vitriolic attacks by students targeting historically marginalized groups (Mangan, 2018b). These perspectives have called for a contemporary re-examination of campus and community values, which will no doubt conflict with extreme perspectives, such as the alt-right and neo-Nazi regimes that espouse beliefs about eugenics and human biodiversity in a pejorative manner.

Campus Preparedness and Responses

For many years, college presidents have expressed an interest in promoting an inclusive society. Yet, the preparedness of this group for a major conflict between free speech and diversity and inclusion draws concern. A recent survey indicates that nearly a majority of college presidents cannot account for their tools to address such a conflict. More directly, when the American Council on Education surveyed college presidents about the significance of promoting an inclusive society welcoming of diverse groups and protecting citizens' free speech rights as important considerations to democracy, the respondents overwhelming supported those statements with 98% indicating either extremely important or very important (Espinosa, Crandall, & Wilkinson, 2018). Notably, 8% more of the college presidents rated inclusion at the highest level of importance relative to free speech rights (see Table 1.1). Interestingly, the preparation to address potentially opposing viewpoints on campus highlighted a lower degree of confidence. Only 51% of the college presidents who responded felt like they had the tools to address conflict on their campus between inclusion and free speech. Twenty-nine percent of the respondents were unsure,

Table 1.1 Responses to Importance of Democratic Values on Campus

"How important do you consider each of the following to be in our democracy?"	Extremely Important	Very Important	Moderately Important
Promoting an inclusive society that is welcoming to diverse groups	82%	16%	2%
Protecting citizens' free speech rights	74%	24%	2%

and 20% of the respondents reported not having the tools necessary to address a conflict.

Campus leadership's legal responses have not always been reasonable, limited to the application of the law, or appropriate for the university's mission. As Fincher (2003) observed, "Legal rationality can easily deteriorate [in higher education] into excessive legalism concerning personnel and program decisions," and he warned that "institutions of higher education can become more concerned with orderly procedure than with substantive justice" (p. 124). Further, campus policies may have extended their reach. For instance, Sun, Hutchens, and Sponsler (2014) explain:

> Critics of student speech and protest policies asserted that in the 1980s, institutional policies put attention on political correctness, whereas in the 2000s, a noticeable shift emerged toward creating policies that address student speech and protest with a focus on public relations.
>
> (p. 1)

Because of uncertainty, reliance on legal heuristics, and public relations, college administrators have, in many instances, limited their courses of action, when addressing tensions of equity, diversity, and inclusion, in favor of focusing solely or primarily on protecting institutional interests (Cole & Harper, 2017), yet legally permissible alternatives are, in many instances, available to address the tensions and are explored throughout this book.

Social Media and Other Messaging Tools

At the center of many of the free speech conflicts is a critical mediator, social media and other messaging tools. For instance, college students have posted, through social media, messages containing racial slurs, mocking groups through animalistic behaviors, and displaying images that strike a historical sign of hate and harm to certain groups (Kerr, 2018). Some colleges, particularly private schools, have opted to take actions under student conduct. Of course, as we established earlier in this chapter, private colleges have more leeway in taking student conduct actions for offensive and harmful expressions. Other colleges have opted to permit the expressions under free speech, especially those messages that fall outside of the boundaries of the educational experiences. Yet, some of the expressions impact the climate of the college, and not all of the posted messages are linked to an identifiable Instagram or Twitter account or blog (Dumont, 2016). Anonymous postings, which over time have been posted through venues such as 4chan, 8chan, Yik Yak, and Whisper, have stirred or escalated tensions on campus.

Social media is also a conduit to generate protest participants. Richard Spencer, a University of Virginia graduate, communicated to his followers via social media and a podcast when he led a May 2017 rally. The basis of the rally was against the City of Charlottesville's plans for removing the Robert E. Lee and Stonewall Jackson statutes in honor of Confederate generals, who served during the American Civil War (Hartocollis, 2017). Drawing on social media to spur on the protest, the events included a march with chants of "You will not replace us," and "Blood and soil."

Social media also generated a second, more noteworthy protest, which took place in August 2017. Known as the "Unite the Right" rally, the protestors included more prominent figures in the white power movement including Ku Klux Klan organizer David Duke. The chants continued including "White Lives Matter," "Hail Trump," and "You Will Not Replace Us!" along with interchanging "Jews Will Not Replace Us!" (Hartocollis, 2017; see also Hemmer, 2019). Social media facilitated the presence of these protestors as well as the counter-protestors. In this encounter, when the protestors met counter-protestors, a brawl started with punching, kicking, and slamming of bodies.

Continuing the effects of social media at the Unite the Right rally, social media illustrates another common practice arising from protests—doxing (Bowles, 2017; Roll, 2017). Social media captured the events and people. Doxxing is the practice of exposing and broadcasting the identities of individuals based on social media postings. In this instance, the doxxing of the white nationalist protestors included where they attended college, with which politicians they had associations, and what evidence demonstrated patterns of civil disobedience in which the identified person had engaged (Bowles, 2017). Doxxing leaves the subsequent actions to the observers to decide what to do. For example, one college community circulated a petition requesting the expulsion of a Unite the Right rally student, and it led another student, who was a leader for the College Republicans chapter at his public college, to step down from that role. Others included posting signs around campus and ostracizing the white nationalist, who protested at the Unite the Right rally.

In short, social media and other messaging tools, which we discuss in greater detail within Chapter 4, offer speed to disseminate information and amplification to increase the number of recipients. At the same time, the rapid pace and volume of information spread makes false and misleading messaging accessible to greater listeners, such as college students, who may choose to act on the information. These factors are significant ones to account for how the environment has changed for contemporary campus protests.

First Amendment Cases

As a general rule, the First Amendment and other free speech related laws (e.g., state contract laws, state defamation laws) often apply to public colleges as they would with other government agencies restricting a person's expressions. These rules do not always align with the mission and priorities of higher education institutions. For instance, the U.S. Supreme Court ruled that the First Amendment may overcome a state claim for intentional infliction of emotional distress (Snyder v. Phelps, 2011). In that case, picketers at a military funeral chanted and displayed placards stating inflammatory messages such as "America is doomed," "You're going to hell," "God hates you," "Fag troops," and "Thank God for dead soldiers." The protestors included members of Westboro Baptist Church in Kansas. According to church representatives, God is angry at the nation and is killing military service members to punish America for condoning homosexuality. The father of the deceased service member whom the funeral was honoring had to endure the offensive, vulgar, and outrageous messages outside his son's funeral. Based on that experience and the physical manifestations that followed such as vomiting and severe depression, he sued the protestors under Maryland's tort law of an intentional infliction of emotional stress. The Supreme Court ruled that when speech is a matter of public concern, it is protected and it trumps laws that would inhibit those expressions. As the Court wrote, "Such speech cannot be restricted simply because it is upsetting or arouses contempt. . . . 'The point of all speech protection . . . is to shield just those choices of content that in someone's eyes are misguided, or even hurtful'" (Snyder v. Phelps, 2011, p. 458). Demonstrating the focus on the constitutional principle over the emotional response, the Court cited an excerpt from another U.S. Supreme Court decision that ruled gay, lesbian, and bisexual descendants of Irish immigrants had a right, under the First Amendment, to process in a St. Patrick's Day parade as an expressive activity (Hurley v. Irish-American Gay, Lesbian, and Bisexual Group, 1995). The Court ruled that when the organizers excluded the group, the organizers violated the group's First Amendment rights by discriminating based on sexual orientation and not complying with Massachusetts' public accommodation law.

Higher education cases involving First Amendment claims follow these legal principles. Even a higher education case that was based a non-First Amendment claim emphasized the special protections under the First Amendment for expressions classified as matters of public concern (Dongguk University v. Yale University, 2013). That case even explained how the case involving the exclusion of the gay, lesbian, and bisexual descendants of Irish immigrants from a parade and the efforts to hold the protestors at the military funeral liable under a claim of intentional infliction of emotional stress would have been improper actions under the First Amendment as emotional harm fails to break down the protective walls of the First Amendment. This reiterated message suggests that the First Amendment is likely to withstand challenges that restrict or discipline college students for offensive, vulgar, and outrageous messages that fall into the category of political and social expressions, which are reasonably classified as matters of public concern. It is also likely, based on other cases, that offensive, vulgar, and outrageous messages that fall within artistic, scientific, and religious expressions receive these special protections under the First Amendment. As the courts rule more inclusively toward protecting free speech—even outside of higher education settings—campus leaders will encounter more changes on acceptable means to educate students, respect free speech, and advance their priorities of diversity and inclusion.

NOTES

1. [We will present illustrations in which intent to target certain groups may produce a penalty enhancement as the courts make reference to hate crimes or statutes. This language will be distinguishable from *per se* hate speech.]
2. The courts have generally accepted this statement *in dictum* from U.S. Supreme Court Justice Potter Stewart. Thus, it carries weight; however, this case was overturned by *Janus v. American Federation* (2018) because the *Abood* case permitted a union agency shop to charge fees to nonunion members. The *Janus* case overruled that policy as violating the First Amendment. This First Amendment policy change does not change the numerous court cases recognizing the special protections associated with social, artistic, literary, and other areas as generally protected under the First Amendment.

REFERENCES

Abood v. Detroit Bd. of Educ., 431 U.S. 209 (1977).

Adams, L. (2017, Oct. 19). Heckling is a staple of controversial campus speeches: Should colleges intervene? *Chronicle of Higher Education*. Retrieved from https://www.chronicle.com/article/Heckling-Is-a-Staple-of/241504

Anti-Defamation League (2018). *White supremacist propaganda on U.S. college campuses rises 77 percent over past nine months: ADL report*. Retrieved from www.adl.org/news/press-releases/white-supremacist-propaganda-on-us-college-campuses-rises-77-percent-over-past

Arizona State University (2019). *Policy statement supporting diversity and free speech*. Tempe, AZ: Committee of Campus Inclusion, Arizona State University. Retrieved from https://inclusion.asu.edu/cci/policies-procedures

Arriaga, A. (2017, Mar. 28). Chapel Hill Replaced KKK Name, but Not the Debate. *Chronicle of Higher Education*. Retrieved from https://www.chronicle.com/article/Chapel-Hill-Replaced-KKK-Name/239609

Barnhardt, C. L. (2014). Campus-based organizing: Tactical repertoires of a contemporary student movement. In C. Broadhurst & G. L. Martin (Eds.), *Radical academia? Understanding the climates for campus activists* (Vol. 167). San Francisco, CA: Wiley.

Bauer-Wolf, J. (2017, September 29). Free speech tour halted at American University. *Inside Higher Ed*. Retrieved from www.insidehighered.com/quicktakes/2017/09/29/free-speech-tour-halted-american-university

Bauman, D. (2018, February 16). After 2016 election, campus hate crimes seemed to jump: Here's what the data tell us. *The Chronicle of Higher Education*. Retrieved from www.chronicle.com/article/After-2016-Election-Campus/242577

Bennett, J. T. (2016). The harm in hate speech: A critique of the empirical and legal bases of hate speech regulation. *Hastings Constitutional Law Quarterly*, *43*(3), 445–536.

Bloucher, J. (2008). Institutions in the marketplace of ideas. *Duke Law Journal*, *57*(4), 821–889.

Board of Regents of University of Wisconsin System v. Southworth, 529 U.S. 217 (2000).

Bowles, N. (2017, August 31). Shaming extremists online becomes a mainstream tool. *New York Times*, B1.

Byrne, J. P. (1990). Racial insults and free speech within the university. *Georgetown Law Journal*, *79*(3), 399–444.

Christian Legal Soc. v. Martinez, 561 U.S. 661 (2010).

Clery Act (Jeanne Clery Disclosure of Campus Security Policy and Campus Crime Statistics Act), 20 U.S.C. § 1092 (2019).

Cole, E. R., & Harper, S. R. (2017). Race and rhetoric: An analysis of college presidents' statements on campus racial incidents. *Journal of Diversity in Higher Education*, *10*(4), 318.

Daniel, P. T. K., Gee, E. G., Sun, J. C., & Pauken, P. D. (2012). *Law, policy, and higher education: Cases and materials*. New Providence, NJ: LexisNexis.

Delegates of the Constitutional Convention (2005). *The Constitution of the United States* (2nd ed). Malta, ID: National Center for Constitutional Studies. (text originated in 1791)

Delgado, R., & Stefancic, J. (2017). Four ironies of campus climate. *Minnesota Law Review*, *101*(5).

Dey, E. L., & Hurtado, S. (1996). Faculty attitudes toward regulating speech on college campuses. *Review of Higher Education*, *20*(1), 15–31.

Dilley, P. (2019). *Gay liberation to campus assimilation: Early non-heterosexual student organizing at Midwestern universities*. Cham, Switzerland: Palgrave MacMillan.

Dirks, N. (2017). Letter to the editor: Violence at Berkley and freedom of speech. *New York Times*. Retrieved from www.nytimes.com/2017/02/03/opinion/violence-at-berkeley-and-freedom-of-speech.html

Dongguk University v. Yale University, 734 F. 3d 113 (2nd Cir. 2013).

Dumont, S. (2016). Campus safety v. freedom of speech: An evaluation of university responses to problematic speech on anonymous social media. *Journal of Business & Technology Law*, *11*(2), 239–264.

Edge, A. (2017, January 28). Two nights on Milo Yiannopoulos's campus tour: As offensive as you'd imagine. *The Guardian*. Retrieved from www.theguardian.com/world/2017/jan/28/milo-yiannopoulos-campus-speaking-tour-colorado

Espinosa, L. L., Crandall, J. R., & Wilkinson, P. (2018). *Free speech and campus inclusion: A survey of college presidents*. Washington, D.C.: American Council on Education.

Fincher, C. (2003). *Administrative leadership: In academic governance and management*. Lanham, MD: University Press of America.

Fish, S. (1994). *There's no such thing as free speech:And it's a good thing, too*. New York, NY: Oxford University Press.

Fisher v. University of Texas, 570 U.S. 297 (2013).

Fogel v. Collins, 531 F. 3d 824 (9th Cir. 2004).

Gallup & Knight Foundation (2018). *Free expression on campus: What college students think about First Amendment issues*. Washington, DC: Gallup, Inc.

Gerlich v. Leath, 861 F. 3d 697 (2017).

Gordon, J., & Johnson, M. (2003). Race, speech, and a hostile educational environment: What color is free speech? *Journal of Social Philosophy*, *34*(3), 414–436. doi:10.1111/1467-9833.00191

Gratz v. Bollinger, 539 U.S. 244 (2003).

Grutter v. Bollinger, 539 U.S. 306 (2003).

Hartocollis, A. (2017, October 17). University of Florida braces for Richard Spencer. *New York Times*. Retrieved from www.nytimes.com/2017/10/17/us/florida-richard-spencer.html

Hazelwood v. Kuhlmeier, 484 U.S. 260 (1988).

Healy v. James, 408 U.S. 169 (1972).

Hemmer, N. (2019, April 26). Opinion: Charlottesville wasn't about Robert E. Lee, Mr. President: It was about racism. *CNN*. Retrieved from www.cnn.com/2019/04/26/opinions/trump-defends-charlottesville-comments-after-biden-video-hemmer/index.html

Herbeck, D. A. (2018). Freedom of speech and the communication discipline: Defending the value of low-value speech. *Communication Education, 67*(2), 245–253. doi:10.1080/03634523.2018.1428760

Hurley v. Irish-American Gay, Lesbian, and Bisexual Group, 515 U.S. 557 (1995).

Hurtado, S. (1992). The campus racial climate: Contexts of conflict. *Journal of Higher Education, 63*(5), 539–569. doi:10.2307/1982093

Husain v. Springer, 494 F. 3d 108 (2nd Cir., 2007).

Hutchens, N. H., & Sun, J. C. (2014). Distinctions under the law between public & private colleges. In J. C. Sun, N. H. Hutchens, & B. A. Sponsler (Eds.), *Responding to campus protests: A practitioner resource* (Legal Links Series) (p. 3). Washington, DC: NASPA-Student Affairs Administrators in Higher Education.

Hutchens, N. H., Sun, J. C., Blanchard, J., & Breslin, J. D. (2014). Employee or student? The First Amendment and student speech arising in practice and internships. *Education Law Reporter, 306*(2), 597–616.

Janus v. American Federation, 138 S. Ct. 2448 (2018).

Keck, T. M. (2016). Hate speech and double standards. *Constitutional Studies, 1*(1), 95–122.

Kerr, E. (2018, January 26). Should students be expelled for posting racist videos? *The Chronicle of Higher Education.* Retrieved from www.chronicle.com/article/Should-Students-Be-Expelled/242364

Lukianoff, G., & Haidt, J. (2015, September). The coddling of the American mind. *The Atlantic.* Retrieved from www.theatlantic.com/magazine/archive/2015/09/the-coddling-of-the-american-mind/399356/

Mangan, K. (2018b, Apr. 12). Seething racial tensions prompt sit-in at Texas State U. student center. *Chronicle of Higher Education.* Retrieved from https://www.chronicle.com/article/Seething-Racial-Tensions/243109

McClurg, J. (2017, July 4). Milo Yiannopoulos' new book is hardly "Dangerous." *USA Today.* Retrieved from www.usatoday.com/story/life/books/2017/07/04/dangerous-milo-yiannopoulos-book-review/103326762/

McMurtrie, B. (2017, Feb. 3). Mayhem at Berkeley hardens new battle lines on free speech. *Chronicle of Higher Education.* Retrieved from https://www.chronicle.com/article/Mayhem-at-Berkeley-Hardens-New/239099

Meiklejohn, A. (1965). *Political freedom: The constitutional powers of the people.* New York, NY: Oxford University Press.

Mill, J.S. (1978). *On Liberty.* Indianapolis, IN: Hackett Publishing.

Milton, J. (1987). Areopagitica. In G. H. Sabine (Ed.), *Areopagitica and of education.* Arlington Heights, IL: Harlan Davidson, Inc.

Moore, W. L., & Bell, J. M. (2017). The right to be racist in college: Racist speech, White institutional space, and the First Amendment. *Law & Policy, 39*(2), 99–120. doi:10.1111/lapo.12076

Orin v. Barclay, 272 F.3d 1207 (9th Cir. 2001).

Papandrea, M. R. (2017). The free speech rights of university students. *Minnesota Law Review, 101*(5), 1801–18.

Papish v. Board of Curators, 410 U.S. 667 (1973).

Patel, V. (2018, May 1). Why a protestor at Chapel Hill doused a confederate monument in red ink and blood. *Chronicle of Higher Education*. Retrieved from https://www.chronicle.com/article/Why-a-Protester-at-Chapel-Hill/243296

Podberesky v. Kirwin, 46 F.3d 5 (4th Cir. 1994).

Post, R. C. (1991). Racist speech, democracy, and the First Amendment. *William and Mary Law Review, 32*(2), 267–327.

Quintana, C. (2018, Jul. 24). Colleges are creating "a generation of sanctimonious, sensitive, supercilious snowflakes," Session says. *Chronicle of Higher Education*. Retrieved from https://www.chronicle.com/article/Colleges-Are-Creating-a/243997

Regents of the University of California v. Bakke, 438 U.S. 265 (1978).

Resnick, G., & Collins, B. (2016, December 29). Milo Yiannopoulos is getting paid big, so will he give away the money he promised? *The Daily Beast*. Retrieved from www.thedailybeast.com/milo-yiannopoulos-is-getting-paid-big-so-will-he-give-away-the-money-he-promised

Rhoads, R. A. (1998). *Freedom's web: Student activism in an age of cultural diversity*. Baltimore, MD: Johns Hopkins University Press.

Rhoads, R. A. (2016). Student activism, diversity, and the struggle for a just society. *Journal of Diversity in Higher Education, 9*(3), 189–202.

Roll, N. (2017, August 15). When your students attend white supremacist rallies. *Inside Higher Ed*. Retrieved from www.insidehighered.com/news/2017/08/15/college-students-unmasked-unite-right-protesters

Rosenberger v. Rector and Visitors of University of Virginia, 515 U.S. 819 (1995).

Slagle, M. (2009). An ethical exploration of free expression and the problem of hate speech. *Journal of Mass Media Ethics, 24*(4), 238–250.

Smith v. Tarrant County Coll. Dist., 694 F. Supp.2d 610 (N.D. Tex. 2010).

Snyder v. Phelps, 562 U.S. 443 (2011).

Southern Poverty Law Center (2000). *Colleges and universities see increase in hate crimes*. Montgomery, AL: Southern Poverty Law Center. Retrieved from www.splcenter.org/fighting-hate/intelligence-report/2000/colleges-and-universities-see-increase-hate-crimes

Southern Poverty Law Center (2017). *White nationalist flyering on American college campuses*. Montgomery, AL: Southern Poverty Law Center. Retrieved from www.splcenter.org/hatewatch/2017/10/17/white-nationalist-flyering-american-college-campuses

State v. Schmid, 423 A.2d 615 (N.J. 1980).

State v. Taupier, 330 Conn. 149 (2018).

Stein, J. (2016, September 15). Milo Yiannopoulus is the pretty, monstrous face of the alt-right: A new force in electoral politics. *Bloomberg Businessweek.* Retrieved from www.bloomberg.com/features/2016-america-divided/milo-yiannopoulos/

Sun, J. C., & Hutchens, N. H. (2014). College students' online speech: Searching for the appropriate standards within First Amendment case principles. *Cardozo Law Review (de-novo), 35,* 129–137.

Sun, J. C., Hutchens, N. H., & Breslin, J. D. (2013). A (virtual) land of confusion with college students' online speech: Introducing the curricular nexus test. *University of Pennsylvania Journal of Constitutional Law, 16*(1), 49–96.

Sun, J. C., Hutchens, N. H., & Sponsler, B. A. (2014). *Responding to campus protests: A practitioner resource* (Legal Links Series). Washington, DC: NASPA-Student Affairs Administrators in Higher Education.

Sweezy v. New Hampshire, 354 U.S. 234 (1957).

Tallentyre, S. G. (2003). *The friends of Voltaire.* Forest Grove, OR: University Press of the Pacific.

Texas v. Johnson, 491 U.S. 397 (1989).

Tinker v. Des Moines School District, 393 U.S. 503 (1969).

Turner, R. (1995). Regulating hate speech and the First Amendment: The attractions of, and objections to, an explicit harms-based analysis. *Indiana Law Review, 29*(2), 257–337.

U.S. Department of Education (2019). *Campus safety and security.* Washington, DC: U.S. Department of Education, Office of Postsecondary Education. Retrieved from https://ope.ed.gov/campussafety/Trend/public/#/answer/2/201/trend/-1/-1/-1/-1

Woodward, B., & Armstrong, S. (1979). *The brethren:Inside the Supreme Court.* New York, NY: Simon & Schuster.

Yeasin v. Durham, 719 Fed. App'x. 844 (2018).

Yiannopoulos, M. (2017). *Dangerous.* Boca Raton, FL: Dangerous Books.

Chapter Two

The Academic Domain
A Relative Deference to Curricular, Classroom, and Learning Experiences

Dean of the School of Education Nick Faust overlooks a sprawling campus of southern classical, Georgian-style buildings. Nestled just west of the Appalachian Mountains, the state university campus and surrounding community honor several Civil War legends who represented the Confederacy, bestowed with named buildings, statutes, and walk-ways. Faust is scheduled to meet with two students, who seek air time with the dean to lodge a complaint. Donna Eberle, Faust's administrative associate, forewarned the dean, "It's about the culture and diversity requirement."

Professor Mahoney, a long-standing member of the education faculty at the public university, teaches the Social Foundations of Education course. It's one of the courses which all education majors must take early-on, and often the only section is with Professor Mahoney. His course covers a wide range of social and cognitive issues taught from insights about the values and impacts of diversity, inclusion, equity, and social justice. The course meets the accreditation standards for a distributed learning experience on diversity, and it also fulfills the university's undergraduate general education requirement of a social justice perspective.

The course fairs well among students with an education major. The evaluations fall around the 60th percentile among well-received courses, but the periodic complaints, with a near visceral reaction from selected students, are not new. In fact, for the ninth time in four years, students have reported to the dean that Professor Mahoney's liberal ideals detract from their learning. If this meeting replicates past reports, the students will, in a nearly scripted fashion, report that they cannot receive a fair evaluation in the course, and they believe Professor Mahoney is discriminating against them for their conservative political views. They will close with the reminder of their academic fears that they must adopt his political beliefs or fail the class.

Professor Mahoney will disagree. He will claim, as he convincingly does each time, that he enjoys the debate of differing perspectives. He will echo his prior assurances, "I am not fearful of dissent. I want the arguments posed to the class. Our students must be prepared for all likely viewpoints so they're ready for their possible placements around the state, which include our rural and urban schools." Professor Mahoney will reiterate, "I simply ask that the arguments presented are reasoned and factual, or we reduce our discussions to ideology, not developmental learning."

This meeting seems insignificant when contextualizing other campus incidents over the past three years such as graffiti containing symbols of hate, speakers espousing White supremacy, an underground group sending "Build that Wall" flyers to the Latinx group, and counter-protestors chanting "White Lives Matter" in response to a Black Lives Matter demonstration following a police shooting of a young Black male. Last week in the School of Education, a group of students in a math education course prepared a project to present a lesson on proportional reasoning and scale factors. It involved measuring Ken and Barbie dolls then measuring their own bodies and placing the measures on the board for public display to examine proportionality and scales with discussions about differences by gender, race, and sexual orientation.

Shaking his head, Dean Faust pauses, moves-on, and calls Ms. Eberle to inquire, "What's Professor Mahoney covering today in his Social Foundations class?" Prepared for the question, Professor Mahoney already informed Eberle that prior to Faust's meeting with the two students, he will be covering critical legal perspectives of southern racial segregation that shaped our country's divided positions. Eberle hands to Faust a stack of readings, including a New Yorker article. He reads a quick excerpt, which highlights legalized and social discrimination practices:

> Seventeen states had laws banning interracial marriage, which is pretty much the heart of the doctrine of white supremacy, until 1967, when the Supreme Court declared them unconstitutional. From the Compromise of 1877, which ended Reconstruction, to the Civil Rights Act of 1964 and the Voting Rights Act of 1965, American race relations were largely shaped by states that had seceded from the Union in 1861, and the elected leaders of those states almost all spoke the language of white supremacy. They did not use dog whistles. "White Supremacy" was the motto of the Alabama Democratic Party until 1966. Mississippi did not ratify the Thirteenth Amendment, which outlawed slavery, until 1995.
>
> (Menand, 2019)

31

Sitting on the couch in his office and reflecting on the campus community of the state university and his obligations to prepare future teachers, Dean Faust stares out his window, which overlooks the quad with the perfectly manicured lawn, pondering, "How do I advance a more nuanced understanding of society today by my students? They're entering an increasingly diverse educational environment, but I am not certain that they're prepared if they've only been exposed to this immediate area and been sheltered on this campus. I must also be responsive to my constituencies, who may need a less progressive, reconstructionist approach to social and demographic changes."

Is learning about expanding horizons or biased to certain features of one view of the horizon? Should learners respond with a logical argument, or does the instructor not appreciate the logic behind the argument because the instructor wishes the learner to conform to certain ideological beliefs? These questions and the scenario above reflect the tension between the learner and instructor when one sees foreclosed opportunities for free speech in the learning environment and another sees expanding one's perspective through educated and reasoned argumentation. This chapter examines the tension between the learner and instructor asking whether the academic decisions exercised by the faculty or the program have stifled students' free speech.

This chapter investigates the notion of professional judgment, which for professors, who are viewed as professional experts, is their academic decisions. Professional experts define their space and operate in it, and our society generally grants deferential authority to them (Abbott, 1988). For instance, judges are the experts over legal analysis; accountants are experts over the measurement and disclosure of financial details; and professors are the experts over their disciplinary studies and academic decisions. According to the courts, academic decisions include the evaluations of satisfactory student progress in areas of study such as medicine (Regents of the University of Michigan v. Ewing, 1985), performance in required clinical experiences in the major (Board of Curators of University of Missouri v. Horowitz, 1978), behaviors in a professional program of study (Al-Dabagh v. Case Western Reserve University, 2015), and the manner in which the curriculum is delivered (Shaikh v. Lincoln Memorial University, 2015). In essence, academic decisions cover the curriculum, which some might define as a "college's or program's mission, purpose, or collective expression of what is important for students to learn" or it might include the "set of experiences that some authorities believe all students should have" (Latucca & Stark, 2009, p. 2). The latter reference to "some authorities" may be an accreditation body, a professional association, or a group of professors in that discipline or department. The point here is that academic decisions include a wide range of activities including the curriculum and the learning performance associated with the curriculum. For the courts, these tend to be sacred ground in which the courts do not interfere.

As a general rule, courts defer to the academic institution to determine the curriculum and the learning environment. It has also been stated in court cases and legal scholarship that academic criteria as manifested through course requirements and assignments generally do not arise to concerns about constitutional rights. This academic deference, which courts oblige, does not suggest that academic decisions must be the best possible option among the choices in order for courts to rule in favor of colleges. One federal judge, not writing for the majority opinion of a case but interjecting thoughts about the line between First Amendment and academic expectations, wrote in a supplementary opinion:

> The bottom line is that when a teacher makes an assignment even if she does it poorly, the student has no constitutional right to do something other than that assignment and receive credit for it. It is not necessary to try to cram this situation into the framework of constitutional precedent, because there is no constitutional question. (Settle v. Dickson County School Board, 1995, pp. 155–156)

This excerpt, while not a legal rule of law, presents a guide to explain the significant deference afforded to academic professionals over college curriculum and learning environments.

The scenario above also illustrates decisions that are related to, but extend beyond the free speech law. For instance, to what extent might the campus and local communities' notable emblems, which pay homage to figures supporting the Confederacy and representing severe discriminatory and racial atrocities, play a role on campus climate and readiness for cultural change? How much weight should the dean place on the number of complaints that the professor received as possibly serving as a pattern, which might be explored further? How do you proceed with interests in balancing academic freedom and commitments to students' voice? Also, how might the dean counsel the professor using the Barbie doll and measuring themselves? How should the professional expectations and standards of a profession shape the curriculum and determine acceptable professional dispositions, competencies, and behaviors?

The scenario also illustrates the growing disconnect between the local community where the college resides and the mindsets of many college students and a much smaller, yet vocal group objecting to educational practices in the U.S. In many instances, a college town does not match the diversity and inclusive climate of a campus. Contextualizing the demographic shifts alone, one only needs to consider the emerging racial composition in the U.S. Demographers forecast significant changes in the population around 2044–2045. At that time, the majority of Americans will no longer be White. Although the largest single category of persons in the U.S. will be non-Hispanic White, for the first time in the nation's history no single group will dominate as representing the majority share of the total number of people living in the nation (Colby & Ortman, 2015; Frey, 2018). This shift has already presented visible tension in terms of community power shifts with significant presence of White nationals and alt-right organizations appearing on college campuses as discussed in Chapter 1.

It is not just the demographics of the students enrolled in higher education that are changing. According to the UCLA 2017 CIRP Freshman Survey, the entering class of first-time, full-time first-year students, who were surveyed from among the nearly 1,500 institutions in the study, reported a political orientation significantly more liberal with 36.2% of the respondents falling within far left or liberal, 41.4% as middle of the road, and 22.4% indicating conservative or far right (Stolzenberg, Eagan, Aragon, Cesar-Davis, Jacobo, Couch, & Rios-Aguilar, 2019). While the latest data, these data do not even show the highest level of liberal leaning college students. The data from 1971 mark one of the highest levels of liberal leaning freshmen in the history of the survey with 40.9% declaring either far left or liberal. "That same year, 15.1% of students described themselves as either 'conservative' or 'far right,' representing the lowest point for these two response categories" (Eagan, Stolzenberg, Ramirez, Aragon, Suchard, & Rios-Aguilar, 2016, p. 26). In 1981, 20.7% of the first-time, full-time first-year students who were surveyed identified their political orientation as far left or liberal, making that the lowest point in time for those combined categories (Eagan et al., 2016). The data are not surprising when considering the context. The 1970s represented an antiwar movement during Vietnam and calls for greater civil rights with college students championing the causes. The 1980s trended the opposite direction where big government was discouraged and private enterprise, especially the banking industry, was fashionably valued with a greater focus on individual wealth and free markets.

While many students self-identified as liberal, examining the political position of college students on specific issues reveals a more centrist tendency. For instance, when asked whether abortion should be legal, 53.2% of centrist students in 1977 agreed or strongly agreed (Eagan et al., 2016). By 2015, that percentage increased to 62.3%. A more pronounced distinction on social ideology occurred on the issue of whether to support legalizing marijuana. In 1972, only 28.6% of the centrists agreed or strongly agreed, but by 2015, that figure increased to 54.1% (Eagan et al., 2016). These mindsets have also changed, though less pronounced, on matters such as support of gay marriage, transgender bathrooms, and gun control. Thus, the data likely forecast more pronounced changes to social issues in the future as these college students will likely become corporate leaders, policymakers, and educators over the next several decades.

Preparing for the future and tackling learning needs for the present, this chapter draws attention to legal and educational principles that shape administrative action toward resolving conflicts between free speech and curriculum that instills diversity and inclusion as fundamental lessons, especially in the helping professions. Accordingly, this chapter examines the expressions and behaviors of college students within the academic domain such as curricular matters, classroom interactions, and other learning environments including internships and field-placements. As noted, the default rule among the courts is that courts tend to grant higher education institutions deference on matters within the academic domain. However, some of the interactions walk a fine line between an academic matter worthy of deference and a political/social expression that affords First Amendment protections. The analyses of the situations rest significantly on the courts' understanding of the situation and the legal framework, which it applies.

TRADITIONAL ACADEMIC SETTINGS

What happens in a classroom or a traditional academic setting stays within the control of the academic instructors. That's what one U.S. Supreme Court case made clear. In *Hazelwood School District v. Kuhlmeier* (1988), a public high school principal removed selected articles, which he objected to, from the final version of the school newspaper. Students wrote the articles as part of a journalism class and featured stories on experiences of teen pregnancy and impacts on teens undergoing parental divorce. The students claimed that the principal violated their First Amendment rights when he censored them by removing their articles. The leadership at the public school disagreed.

Because the principal worked at a public school and acted in his official capacity, the law considers his actions as on behalf of the government. Given that, questions of the First Amendment are appropriate in this instance. Specifically, the legal issue for this case addresses "the extent to which [public school] educators may exercise editorial control over the contents of a high school newspaper produced as part of the school's journalism curriculum" (p. 262). More broadly, the legal issue has application beyond a high school and editorial control over a newspaper. The case also represents whether a public educational institution may place restrictions on student speech when it involves school-sponsored expressive activities such as learning in the classroom or other academic settings. In other words, if a public school is going to speak, which it does through its curriculum, the curricular or learning environment does not become open for protest like a public park, a campus free speech zone, or other spaces on campus.

The U.S. Supreme Court made clear that a public school may place restrictions on student speech in certain instances. The Court expressed that when the matter "concerns educators' authority over school-sponsored publications, theatrical productions, and other expressive activities that students, parents, and members of the public might reasonably perceive to bear the imprimatur of the school" then the public school has a right to exercise its authority and place reasonable restrictions (p. 271). The Court continued to describe that

> activities, [which] may fairly be characterized as part of the school curriculum, whether or not they occur in a traditional classroom setting, so long as they are supervised by faculty members and designed to impart particular knowledge or skills to student participants and audiences

are afforded greater latitude and fall within the purview of the educators right to place reasonable restrictions on students' speech (p. 271).

The Supreme Court ruled that the instructional environment or the academic setting is not a public forum where students and other members of the college community may exercise free speech. Simply stated, the academic setting, which may be instruction in a classroom, a theatrical play for course credit, or a lab for experiential learning, is not traditional or designated fora in which a student may express freely under the guise of the First Amendment. Instead, in the academic setting,

> [e]ducators [at public colleges] are entitled to exercise . . . control over . . . student expression to assure that participants learn whatever lessons the activity is designed to teach, that readers or listeners are not exposed to material that may be inappropriate for their level of maturity, and that the views of the individual speaker are not erroneously attributed to the school.
>
> (p. 271)

Presenting the legal rule, the Court declared that educators may have rights to editorial "control over the style and content of student speech in school-sponsored expressive activities so long as their actions are *reasonably related to legitimate pedagogical concerns*" (emphasis added) (p. 273).

Let's not confuse this case with the *Tinker* case, which is discussed in Chapters 1 and 3. In *Tinker*, students were silently protesting the Vietnam War by wearing black armbands. Because the expression represented "political speech," the speech itself receives special protections. The students happened to make their silent protest on campus, but it also occurred wherever else they wore the bands (e.g., on the school bus, outside of the campus) and it was not disruptive. Given this mix of circumstances (e.g., symbolic political expression that was not disruptive), the U.S. Supreme Court raised the issue of whether the First Amendment requires a public "school to tolerate particular student speech" such as a silent protest using symbolic speech (Hazelwood School District v. Kuhlmeier, 1988, p. 271).

The *Tinker* case decision held schools cannot regulate political speech that students conveyed through a silent protest unless it creates a substantial disruption. In *Hazelwood*, it was slightly (but significantly) different. This case addressed whether the First Amendment requires a public school to affirmatively promote particular student speech. That is, if a student wants to convey something on campus, does the public school have to promote that message? The answer is "No." An academic setting in which curricular learning activity is taking place is not a forum for free expression. Students wishing to express themselves, particularly at public institutions, may move to other settings. A public school is not required to support the student from promoting whatever the student wants, and the college may restrict the expressions.

Besides discussions or interactions within a class, an assignment (e.g., a research paper, a business plan), presentation (e.g., research study presentation, role-playing activity), or another academic submission is generally not a public forum for one to express freely. Accordingly, even a seemingly unstructured assignment or a voluntary section to an assignment such as an acknowledgment section to a thesis allows a public college to place boundaries.

In *Brown v. Li* (2002), a student inserted a "Disacknowledgments" section after his thesis committee had signed and approved the primary portion of the document. The "Disacknowledgments" section opened with: "I would like to offer special [F@*$] You's to the following degenerates for of being an ever-present hindrance during my graduate career" (p. 943). He identified the dean and staff of the university's graduate school, the staff at the university library, and a former California governor. The latter was included because the University of California tuition went up. The student's thesis committee did not accept the thesis once they learned about the "Disacknowledgments" section. The committee withheld granting the degree, and placed the student on academic probation for failing to complete the degree in a timely manner. Eventually, the university relented and

37

gave him the degree, as he had completed all degree requirements except submission of the approved thesis to the library. Nonetheless, the student filed suit based on free speech rights under the First Amendment. A federal appellate court ruled that the student's disacknowledgments were not protected under the First Amendment. The court's decision offers several important points as guidance for campus leaders. First, the court emphasized that it defers to the authority of educational institutions to establish its curricular standards. The court stated that "an educator can, consistent with the First Amendment, require that a student comply with the terms of an academic assignment" (p. 949). The law grants the leeway needed for college educators as "the First Amendment does not require an educator to change the assignment to suit the student's opinion or to approve the work of a student that, in his or her judgment, fails to meet a legitimate academic standard" (p. 949). Second, the court made a clear distinction between curricular and extracurricular activities in higher education.

> The Supreme Court has suggested that core *curricular* speech—that which is an integral part of the classroom teaching function of an educational institution—differs from students' *extracurricular* speech and that a public educational institution retains discretion to prescribe its curriculum.
>
> (p. 950)

While this chapter focuses on curricular matters, in short, the court is making clear that curricular matters are treated differently for free speech purposes, and the deferential treatment is significant over curricular and course-based learning matters. Third, the court informed us that the *Hazelwood* case, which is discussed above, offers a significant legal source for situations such as this one. It observed that "committee members acted well within their discretion, and in conformity with the First Amendment, when they declined to approve the noncompliant section" (p. 952). Specifically, the court concluded that the committee's decision was "reasonably related to a legitimate pedagogical objective: teaching [the graduate student] the proper format for a scientific paper" (p. 952). In other words, an academic unit should examine (i) the academic committee or instructor's reasoning for restricting the student's expression or behavior and (ii) determine if that reasoning is "reasonably related to a legitimate pedagogical objective." Fourth, while the application of this case clearly applies to acknowledgements and dedications for student theses or dissertations, this case also illuminates potential application in other settings. For instance, this case may apply to a report or paper preface, addenda, and footnotes. Finally, this student's experience and behavior might be an outlier and properly be cast away. At the same time, it is possible this action might signal to campus leaders that there are problems beyond a student's nonconformance with the academic standards of an assignment. The behavior might, through an inquiry, shed light on graduate education, student services, or more broadly, the campus climate for students. Thus, these incidents, while perplexing at times, may serve as useful indicators of students' experiences representing a small group or a widespread concern.

The reasoning from the "Disacknowledgments" case also held true for a case involving a student's writing assignments. The instructor of the class, English 380: Advanced Critical Writing, had placed guidelines for free writing activities. For instance, the instructor suggested that students incorporate "New vocabulary defined and used in a sentence," "Passages of interest from each reading assignment, with an explanation," "Responses to all EE ["*The Eloquent Essay*"—one of the required course texts] and King [Stephen King's "*On Writing: A Memoir of the Craft* "—another required text] readings," "Observation logs: People, places, etc.," and "Creative entries of your own." One student in the course chose to make use of the free writing opportunity to pen an essay entitled "Hot for Teacher" in which he referenced his sexual attraction to the instructor. He wrote:

> Then there's Ms. Mitzelfeld. English 380. She walks in and I say to myself "Drop, motherfucker, drop." Kee—Rist, I'll never learn a thing. Tall, blond, stacked, skirt, heels, fingernails, smart, articulate, smile. I'm toast but I stay. I'll fuck up my whole Tuesday—Thursday class thing if I drop. I'll search for something unattractive about her. No luck yet. Shit.
> (Corlett v. Oakland University Board of Trustees, 2013, p. 799)

These writings continued with his fetish of relating the instructor to a seductive television character. The court ruled that the student's work was not protected under the First Amendment and belonged within the ordinary purview of the college instructor, who has oversight of the curriculum and course content.

The college writing instructor's permissibility to limit a student's expressions based on curricular grounds could also apply to other academic situations that challenge a college's diversity and inclusion priority. The examples extend far beyond a writing course. For instance, a student might construct a policy brief for a public affairs class recommending state sanctioned extinction of Black gang members through forms of violence, alter a play script that infuses derogatory scenes targeted at a Latinx population, propose a business plan directed at bankrupting Asian grocery store owners, or construct a product for a mechanical engineering class that appears, only for aesthetic purposes, to reflect a swastika. In these situations, the instructor or academic program may not accept the assignments if there is a showing that the non-acceptance is reasonably related to a legitimate pedagogical objective.

The analysis for college instructors and campus leaders draws on four areas to analyze these types of concerns.

1. How does the activity meet the requirements of the assignment and learning objectives? Does the academic experience calls for design, content, or analyses that would be appropriate for such learning deliverables? If the assignment does not meet the stated requirements and learning objectives and the instructions do not present reasonable justifications based on design, content, or analyses, it is likely that the assignment may be restricted and unacceptable.

2. Is the restriction reasonably related to a legitimate pedagogical objective? If the instructor's justification for restricting the student's expression or behavior is reasonably related to a legitimate pedagogical objective, then the assignment may be properly restricted and unacceptable for the academic setting.

3. Is there a law or college policy that would otherwise protect the assignment? Might there be a special provision for students' academic freedom or a special state law that blocks faculty from exercising their rights in this instance? If there is a law or college policy that would preclude restrictions such as a professional standard for licensure or certification, it is possible that the assignment may be permitted. At the same time, there may be a college policy, such as a harassment policy, which serves as additional support for classifying the assignment or learning activity as unacceptable.

4. May the restriction be seen as discriminatory pretext for punishing the student based on race, color, national origin, gender, age, religion, or political/ideological perspective? Discrimination based on protected classes (e.g., race, gender, age, and religion) or political viewpoint or ideology is impermissible and presents potential legal challenges at public colleges under First Amendment for free speech and Fourteenth Amendment for equal protection. In addition, colleges that receive federal dollars may be subject to Title VI of the Civil Rights Act of 1964 for race, color, and national origin discrimination and Title IX of the Educational Amendments of 1972 for sex/gender-based discrimination. If such evidence of discrimination emerges, the college would be required to produce evidence that the decision was not based on one of the enumerated discriminatory reasons or had a compelling governmental interest to overcome the

discriminatory basis along with a showing that the action was narrowly tailored so it only met the intended governmental interest and not more.

The discussion above presented courts' deferential treatment of matters involving academic decisions, which typically pertain to curricular, learning environment matters, or academic performance. Of course, not all professors or instructors present relevant material or initiate appropriate discussions, which create a non-inclusive campus environment. For instance, in *Hardy v. Jefferson Community College* (2001), a foul-mouthed professor used racially and sexually vulgar words in class. A federal appellate court ruled that speech that was not "germane to the subject matter" was not protected. Further, courts today might assert that a professor's speech is pursuant to one's official duties as a faculty member so there is no constitutional protection over those expressions (Hutchens & Sun, 2013). According to *Garcetti v. Ceballos* (2006), when "public employees make statements pursuant to their official duties, the employees are not speaking as citizens for First Amendment purposes, and the Constitution does not insulate their communications from employer discipline" (p. 421). This rule, which has never been applied to the college professor's role as a classroom teacher, may one day be considered for the classroom setting. While an instructor's utterance may be at issue, possible routes for analysis are available such as expressions which are not germane to the subject matter are not afforded protection.

What is less clear is what happens when an instructor's past comes to light and it creates an unsafe or vulnerable feeling for students. In *Levin v. Harleston* (1992), Professor Michael Levin wrote three published works that were denigrating of Blacks. Students found out, so the dean created a shadow section, which ran during parallel times so students who wanted to transfer out of Levin's class could do so. According to the court record, no student ever complained that Levin treated students unfairly based on race. Nonetheless, the college created the shadow section based on the belief that "Professor Levin's expression of his theories outside the classroom harmed the students and the educational process within the classroom" (Levin v. Harleston, 1992, p. 88). The college created an advisory committee to determine if Levin's academic freedom protected him or his writings represented misconduct. In light of the situation, Levin sued under free speech and due process rights. The federal appellate court sided with Levin that the college failed to produce evidence of Levin's harm to students or the educational process arising from his writings. Fast-forward to 2019, when students at the University of Alabama at Birmingham called a teaching assistant a Nazi because of his affiliation with Identity Evropa, a recognized White nationalist group concerned with raising the White racial consciousness (Vasquez, 2019). According to a news article in *The Chronicle of Higher Education*, the teaching assistant reports that he has never had a bias complaint during his seven years in that role. Further, there is no evidence of conduct violations. But, how will students respond to this situation and will it lead to evidence of harm onto students or their educational process? Only time will tell, and perhaps, an incident stirring campus tensions around inclusion and learning.

PROFESSIONAL STANDARDS AND CERTIFICATIONS

Professional standards leading to licensure and certification within education, counseling, social work, and other fields have also been challenged over the past decade over allegations that the academic requirements in these fields have quashed students' free speech, unfairly evaluating students' performance and inhibiting free exercise of religion. Often, these cases have emerged as a contest between the student and institution over requirements for diversity and inclusion awareness and multicultural competencies. In *Head v. Board of Trustees* (2008), a former student sued San Jose State University and university faculty and administrators under several claims, notably accusing the public university of violating his First Amendment free speech rights. Stephen Head was enrolled in a Secondary Education Department's Teacher Credential Program at San Jose State University. The basis of his suit was the student's objection to the university's requirement that he take a course in multiculturalism, which he failed. He argued that "he was forced to adopt 'predetermined radical leftist or otherwise socially controversial viewpoints' that are counter to his conservative positions" (Head v. Board of Trustees, 2008, p. 8). The federal appellate court concluded that the course requirement did not amount to a free speech violation. It was unconvinced that a course, or even how this particular course was structured, compromised Head's personal rights. In fact, the court struggled to find a legal claim as Head simply asserted that he was not allowed to fully discuss certain topics "to the full extent he sought and that he was once criticized by the instructor for his political views." The court held his treatment simply related to learning the course material and the reasoning and was not discriminatory based on his political ideology (Head v. Board of Trustees, 2006, 2008).

The conflict between political ideology and curricular goals that align with professional standards is not new, especially when embedding the perspectives of diversity and inclusion. Nonetheless, the research is well established that infusion of diversity into college learning spurs on significantly positive effects for nearly all students (Gurin, Dey, Hurtado, & Gurin 2002;

Gurin, Dey, Gurin, & Hurtado, 2003; Milem, Chang, & Antonio, 2005; Sáenz, Ngai, & Hurtado, 2007). For instance, drawing from data of 2,974 college students at 19 four-year and two-year colleges with a liberal arts focus, college students engaged in interactional and classroom diversity lead to higher levels of social and political activism. This impact is significant for students who self-identify as politically on the far right, conservative, or middle of the road. "For these students[,] the net effects of classroom diversity experiences were substantially larger, positive, and statistically significant" (Pascarella, Salisbury, Martin, & Blaich, 2012, p. 486). Students' agency and empowerment are positive outcomes, and our role as educators should affirm such behaviors, when appropriately placed and demonstrated.

The learning effects and mindsets also lead to positive educational outcomes. Drawing on a longitudinal sample of 8,475 first-year students at 46 institutions, Bowman (2014) finds that openness to diversity significantly relates to other key learning activities and values. For instance, these students are more inclined to interact with faculty and staff. The students are more likely to seek out high quality peer interactions as part of the learning process. Also, these students express greater value toward good teaching–learning practices in the classroom.

Bowman's study (2014) also reveals another interesting finding for educators who value diversity and inclusion. He observes that the openness to diversity and openness to challenge are intertwined reflecting a single construct. "Because diversity experiences often involve challenge—particularly for students who have had limited exposure to people different from themselves—it seems unlikely that a student would be open to diversity but not open to challenge, or vice-versa" (Bowman, 2014, p. 287). In other words, openness to diversity has greater impacts for learning agility, leadership, and innovation, which maintain constructs around openness to challenge.

In the professional fields, the openness to diversity and openness to challenge are also important factors to practice. Yet, as the cases below illustrate, the openness levels and understanding of another person's perspective have been re-interpreted by some students as forcefully adopting a perspective or orientation. Generally speaking, the academic and professional standards and evidence of professional competence are not intended to adopt the client or student's perspective or orientation, but understand them. As one study on social work diversity standards explained,

> Acknowledging and legitimizing student experiences does not necessarily mean changing what is taught in the classroom. In some instances it may, but it may require more[]so that educators change how they relate to conservative students. The challenge will be

43

> responding to conservative students without being defensive or reactive, and without compromising social work values or ethics.
>
> (Fram & Miller-Cribbs, 2008, p. 895)

Likewise, professional standards seek to take the lens of the client, which also requires bracketing our own positions about persons and situations. To that end, the American Counseling Association presents professional standards so that counseling students and professionals in the field "value the diversity of clients across sexual orientation, age, culture, disability, ethnicity, race, religion/spirituality, gender, gender identity, marital status/ partnership, language preference, and socioeconomic status" not necessarily adopt them (Kaplan, 2012, p. 143). The cases below illustrate the tensions, raise legal issues, and present a practice-based approach on resolving the contested matter.

Learning and Professional Standards Conflicting With Religion

Religious, political, and ideological beliefs often shape the students' dialectic engagement and behaviors in academic settings. Yet, how does an academic program respond when religious beliefs make professional practice within an academic program difficult or impossible to perform? One case, *Keeton v. Anderson-Wiley* (2011), demonstrates the challenge in a counselor education program.

Jennifer Keeton was enrolled in a counselor education program at public university. According to court documents, Keeton expressed that she is "a Christian who is committed to the truth of the Bible, including what she believes are its teachings on human nature, the purpose and meaning of life, and the ethical standards that govern human conduct" (Keeton v. Anderson-Wiley, 2011, p. 864). In particular, she asserted

> Sexual behavior is the result of personal choice for which individuals are accountable, not inevitable deterministic forces; that gender is fixed and binary (i.e., male or female), not a social construct or personal choice subject to individual change; and that homosexuality is a "lifestyle," not a "state of being."
>
> (p. 864)

Based on a series of interactions between Keeton and her professors, it became apparent that Keeton "believed that the GLBTQ population suffers from identity confusion, and that she intended to attempt to convert students from being homosexual to heterosexual" (p. 868). When discussing

44

a hypothetical about counseling a high school student in crisis after questioning his sexual orientation, Keeton revealed that she "would tell the student that it was not okay to be gay" (p. 868). Keeton also shared with a classmate in the program that

> if a client discloses that he is gay, . . . [she would] tell the client that his behavior is morally wrong and then try to change the client's behavior, and if she were unable to help the client change his behavior, she would refer him to someone practicing conversion therapy. (p. 869)

In light of these events, the academic program faculty placed Keeton on a remediation plan to address their concerns about her "ability to be a multiculturally competent counselor, particularly with regard to working with gay, lesbian, bisexual, transgender, and queer/questioning (GLBTQ) populations" (p. 867). The plan was necessary to demonstrate Keeton may exhibit one of the practice standards for counselors, and it presented a legitimate pedagogical concern in teaching its students to comply with the American Counseling Association's ACA Code of Ethics. Yet, rather than consenting to the plan, Keeton sued primarily under the First Amendment based on free speech and free exercise of her religion.

Keeton asserted that the state university imposed the remediation plan in reaction to her views about homosexuality. If true, that outcome would have likely led to a viable claim against the state university for violating her free exercise of religion. After examining the record, the evidence demonstrated that the public university placed Keeton on the remediation plan because she indicated that she would "impose her personal religious views on her clients, in violation of the ACA Code of Ethics" (p. 872). The purpose of the plan, which had a legitimate pedagogical purpose, "was to teach her how to effectively counsel [LGBTQ] clients in accordance with the ACA Code of Ethics" (p. 872). Thus, the federal appellate court ruled that Keeton's free speech rights under the First Amendment had not been infringed upon and it supported the implementation of Keeton's remediation plan.

When academics do not draw on professional judgment, the case analysis shifts slightly. The case *Ward v. Polite* (2012) illustrates this situation. Julea Ward was enrolled in a graduate counseling program at Eastern Michigan University in hopes of becoming a school counselor. Until her practicum, she did well in the program holding a 3.91 grade point average. During Ward's practicum experience, she was asked to counsel a gay client. Because of her Christian faith, she requested her faculty supervisor "either to refer the client to another student or to permit her to begin counseling and make a referral if the counseling session turned to relationship issues" (Ward v. Polite, 2012,

p. 730). Following the event, the university conducted a disciplinary hearing and eventually expelled her. Ward sued the university based on alleged constitutional violations under the First and Fourteenth Amendments.

The initial trial court ruled in favor for Eastern Michigan University. The federal appellate court reversed the decision and sent it back to the trial court to examine some factual question. Nonetheless, while doing so, the federal appellate court emphasized how "[c]urriculum choices are a form of school speech, giving schools considerable flexibility in designing courses and policies and in enforcing them so long as they amount to reasonable means of furthering legitimate educational ends" (Ward v. Polite, 2012, p. 730). Eastern Michigan University voiced its curriculum choices. It had a policy that prohibited students from discriminating against others based on sexual orientation. The counseling program also instructed students to affirm a client's values during counseling sessions.

The court supported the university's position, which included the anti-discrimination policy. It also acknowledged the practicum class experience as an academic requirement and the support for the client's values. However, it pointed out the discrepancy between the university's policy and the professional standards. The appellate court drew attention to a few noteworthy responses gathered during the deposition stage of the case. For instance, one of the professors in the program asked Ward if she would "'see [her] brand of Christianity as superior to' that of a Christian client who viewed her faith differently" (p. 737). Another professor questioned "how someone with such strong religious beliefs [as Ward's] would enter a profession that would cause [her] to go against those beliefs . . . by its stated code of ethics" (pp. 737–738). A third professor challenged Ward

> asking whether she believed that "anyone [is] more righteous than another before God?" and whether, if Ward's stated beliefs were true, "doesn't that mean that you're all on the same boat and shouldn't [gays and lesbians] be accorded the same respect and honor that God would give them?"
>
> (p. 738)

The record raised some concerns about potential pretext for religious discrimination. Based on the appellate court review, there were more questions left unanswered. The appellate court, which only reviews questions of legal policy and not challenges about factual questions over the evidence or expert testimony, sent back the case to the trial court to determine fact-finding on several issues. First, it raised concerns whether the American Counseling Association's ethics code actually prohibits the exercise of values-based referrals as Ward requested. The appellate court asked: "What exactly did Ward do wrong in making the referral request?" (Ward v. Polite, 2012, p. 735). Second, the court inquired whether the public university had any written policy that would bar a graduate student studying counseling from requesting a referral based on faith-based justifications, specifically to investigate if this instance was pretext to punish the student based on her religious views. Third, the court needed the responses to investigate whether the public university had a compelling governmental interest in Ward's academic dismissal from the counseling program because of her use of the referral. At the end, Eastern Michigan and Julea Ward settled the case, which was a three-year ordeal (Rudow, 2013).

This case was significant to the counseling profession. Although the appellate court remanded the case for more factual findings, this case illustrates that "courts are more reluctant to defer to certification decisions based on officials' personal disagreement with a student's views" (Oyama v. University of Hawaii, 2015, p. 866). Instead, courts search for professional standards to draw upon as the basis for acceptable academic and professional judgments, and of course, it would not expect perceived religious hostility as a retort to a student's performance. Also, the counseling profession and educators have a challenging task of educating non-professionals including the legal community and policymakers about the counseling profession. David Kaplan testified as an expert witness representing the American Counseling Association. During that testimony, he explained how the profession takes the lens of the client, not the counselor (Kaplan, 2014). Framing the counselor's role, a *New York Times* article interview of American Civil Liberties Union lawyer Daniel Mach captured an underlying problem with many of the briefs submitted against Eastern Michigan University. "[M]any of the briefs fail[ed] to investigate . . . the role of the counselor or therapist" (Oppenheimer, 2012, p. A18). The analysis raised a seemingly rhetorical or ethical question: "Is it to 'affirm' the client's beliefs, or to offer support and guidance, even to clients whose practices one may find distasteful or morally wrong?" (Oppenheimer, 2012, p. A18). Finally, the counseling educators and other helping professions such as teachers and social workers should continue making the distinction one's inability to perform based on preparation and experience versus one's unwillingness to perform supports or services in spite of a professional obligation (Kaplan, 2014).

Professional Standards and Conflicting Ideological Perspectives

The professional standards and principles may conflict with students' non-religious ideological stances. This conflict also may impact educational experiences leading to entry into a professional field. A case, *Oyama v.*

47

University of Hawaii (2015), illustrates a public university's permissible exercise of its curricular decisions by drawing heavily on professional standards.

Mark Oyama was in a graduate secondary education program, and he was applying to be a student teacher, which is the practice-based component of the academic experience. Among the goals of the program, a candidate must demonstrate being a knowledgeable, effective, and caring professional. According to the student handbook, a caring candidate for the teaching professions seeks to "advanc[e] social justice and overcom[e] both discrimination and oppression" and "requires a high level of professionalism demonstrated through ethical behavior, competence, reflection, fairness, respect for diversity, and a commitment to inclusion and social responsibility" (Oyama v. University of Hawaii, 2015, p. 855). This area presented difficulties for Oyama.

A series of dispositional concerns emerged about his Oyama's ability to care for students. For instance, he expressed in an assignment and to a professor that he believes in adult-child sexual relations. He asserted that the "age of consent should be either 0, or whatever age a child is when puberty begins" (p. 856). He even expressed his approval if a 12-year-old student had a sexual relationship with a teacher. Although he would report the relationship pursuant to the law, he did not see any problem with it. Further, he opposed any effort to mainstream a student with a disability that is "sufficiently severe and not of a physical nature" (p. 856). According to Oyama, that inclusion would provide little benefit to the student with a disability and a secondary education teacher should not be required to have the skill sets to manage this educational environment. He also espoused that 90% of the special education students who he encountered were "fakers." He did not believe they had the diagnosed disabilities, and he opined that some may be "medically-based neurological conditions" (p. 857).

Oyama's dispositions aligned with his actions in the field experiences during his academic program. His evaluations consisted of several "unacceptable" evaluation scores. Notably, he failed to meet standards with his "ability to teach effectively, work collaboratively with colleagues, respond to suggestions from supervisors, and demonstrate the level of professionalism expected of middle school teachers" (p. 857). Given the dispositions coupled with his evaluations, Oyama's student teaching application was denied. He claimed that his personal opinions were the basis of the denial. Yet, the public university drew on two sets of professional standards from Hawaii and national regulations about Oyama's remarks and dispositions. The first set of professional standards addressed the prohibiting of sexual contact between teachers and students or minors and the obligation that teachers take all reasonable precautions to protect student safety. The second set of regulations countered Oyama's position about support students with disabilities. The public university presented a regulation intended to avoid discrimination of students with disabilities by affording them opportunities to learn through differentiated forms of instruction. It also cited compliance with the Individuals with Disabilities Education Act (2015), which affords students with disabilities free appropriate public education tailored to their needs. Collectively, these professional standards and regulations demonstrated how Oyama was not fit to serve as a secondary school teacher because Oyama's "statements indicated that he had not absorbed, and likely would not comply with, defined and established standards for the teaching profession" (Oyama v. University of Hawaii, 2015, p. 870).

Not all the court cases draw on a public college's ability to restrict a student's expression through the lens of whether the restrictions are reasonably related to a legitimate pedagogical objective. A series of cases have inquired about the mandates for the professional field, particularly for licensure or certification. The *Oyama* case illustrates that approach. This case recognized a level of deference to the academic unit as the certifying entity by presenting these considerations, which serve as a guide to campus leaders.

1. Courts often defer to academic decisions of curricular and course learning when the structure and principles are based on the professional standards articulated for licensure or certification "and not on officials' personal disagreement with students' views" (Oyama v. University of Hawaii, 2015, pp. 867–868) (see also Axson-Flynn v. Johnson, 2004; Tatro v. University of Minnesota, 2012).

2. The professional standards employed and the evaluation system in place to determine the candidate's suitability into the profession must be clearly aligned and present the basis for its decision to assert the academic consequences such as not allowing a student to proceed into a student teaching placement or not meeting certification requirements.

3. The public college's restrictions must be narrowly tailored to the context of meeting the specific goals of the professional standards.

4. Further, the application of the professional standards is limited to the specific roles and responsibilities of the profession, not other areas of the academic experience.

5. The academic decision makers in these cases must demonstrate the exercise of reasonable professional judgment.

Sound Professional Judgment

Similarly, for private colleges, the courts are interested in the professional standards and exercise of sound professional judgment. *Al-Dabagh v. Case Western Reserve University* (2015) illustrates this application.

Amir Al-Dabagh was a medical student at Case Western Reserve University. He performed well academically, except his professionalism was lacking. He was late to nearly 30% of his discussion sessions during his first year in medical school. The university also had two reports of females complaining about his sexual misbehavior, which included an allegation of Al-Dabagh's unwanted sexual proposition and a grabbing of a female's butt.

The behaviors escalated into the curricular and learning environment through Al-Dabagh's performance on his internal medicine internship. According to the federal appellate court, "Nurses and hospital staffers 'consistently complained about his demeanor'" (Al-Dabagh v. Case Western Reserve University, 2015, p. 358). In at least one instance, "a patient's family 'kicked him out of the room'" and reports that he "sometimes gave patient-status presentations without first preparing" (p. 358). His record of unprofessionalism consisted of a detailed addendum, a student record process that the medical school never had to use on another student within the prior 25 years. The tipping point for the administrators to end Al-Dabagh's medical school enrollment was when he was convicted for driving while intoxicated. That event triggered an emergency session of the medical school's Committee on Students to conduct a review, which unanimously denied certifying Al-Dabagh for graduation and his academic dismissal.

Al-Dabagh sued the private university under contract law claiming that the university breached its duties of good faith and fair dealing when it declined to award him the degree. When examining a breach of duty of good faith and fair dealing, a court examines the interactions and the decisions to determine whether the university acted arbitrarily and capriciously in its decision to dismiss the student. As a practical matter, the court is examining if the private university exercised professional judgment or if the decision was a substantial departure from accepted academic norms. It is worth noting that this same analysis is also employed when there is a constitutional challenge based on Fourteenth Amendment due process over the evaluation or factors for determination in an academic dismissal (Regents of the University of Michigan v. Ewing, 1985).

In this case, the Committee on Students reviewed Al-Dabagh's professionalism evaluation drawing on multiple instances of poor academic performance for clinical experiences, and they exercised academic judgment to make its determination. Consistent with the other cases discussed above, a university, whether private or public, has significant control over curricular matters.

CONCLUDING REMARKS

Uncovering the various legal and educational principles that undergird tensions between free speech and the diversity and inclusion priority, this chapter presented the lessons emergent from the academic setting—including curricular decisions and the class-based learning environment. These lessons lead to three practice-based considerations.

1. **Deference to Academics:** Courts typically afford great deference to the academic community over curricular and learning matters. To ensure the respect of the academic deference, faculty must demonstrate sound professional judgment based on a clear basis for their reasoning. It is advisable that the faculty conduct a systematic and consistent review and may demonstrate a decision that was made conscientiously and with careful deliberation drawing on evaluation of the student's academic record.

2. **Beyond the Classroom, But not Beyond Academic Setting:** Courts separate the academic and disciplinary settings. The significant message is that courts generally give lots of discretion to challenges that impact the academic program (e.g., in the classroom, on a thesis, in a play as a part of an acting class) as opposed to behavioral matters that are not associated with an academic program (e.g., behaviors in the residence hall, intramurals, cafeteria, or at the student union). Thus, campus leaders should place parameters on what are curricular-based or learning sourced matters, which sometimes are blended in professional education settings. Yet, the distinction helps courts delineate the analysis.

3. **Consideration of Suspect Indicators:** Red flags are raised with the courts when evidence of certain complaints arises. As one court noted, "like judges, teachers should not punish or reward people on the basis of inadmissible factors—race, religion, gender, political ideology—but teachers, like judges, must daily decide which arguments are relevant, which computations are correct, which analogies are good or bad, and when it is time to stop writing or talking" (Settle v. Dickson County School Board, 1995, pp. 155–156). Accordingly, academic staff interactions must demonstrate neutral expressions, especially when religious or political justifications are asserted.

51

REFERENCES

Abbott, A. (1988). *The system of professions: An essay on the division of expert labor*. Chicago, IL: The University of Chicago Press.

Al-Dabagh v. Case Western Reserve University, 777 F.3d 355 (6th Cir. 2015).

Axson-Flynn v. Johnson, 356 F.3d 1277 (10th Cir. 2004).

Board of Curators of University of Missouri v. Horowitz, 435 U.S. 78 (1978).

Bowman, N. A. (2014). Conceptualizing openness to diversity and challenge: Its relation to college experiences, achievement, and retention. *Innovative Higher Education, 39*(4), 277–291. doi:10.1007/s10755-014-9281-8

Brown v. Li. 308 F.3d 939 (9th Cir. 2002).

Colby, S. L., & Ortman, J. M. (2015). *Projections of the size and composition of the U.S. population: 2014 to 2060*. Washington, D.C.: U.S. Census Bureau.

Corlett v. Oakland University Board of Trustees, 958 F. Supp. 2d 795 (E.D. Mich. 2013).

Eagan, M. K., Stolzenberg, E. B., Ramirez, J. J., Aragon, M. C., Suchard, M. R., & Rios-Aguilar, C. (2016). *The American freshman: Fifty-year trends, 1966–2015*. Los Angeles, CA: Higher Education Research Institute, UCLA.

Fram, M. S., & Miller-Cribbs, J. (2008). Liberal and conservative in social work education: Exploring student experiences. *Social Work Education, 27*(8), 883–897.

Frey, W. H. (2018). *The US will become "minority white" in 2045, census projects*. Retrieved from www.brookings.edu/blog/the-avenue/2018/03/14/the-us-will-become-minority-white-in-2045-census-projects/

Garcetti v. Ceballos, 547 U.S. 410 (2006).

Gurin, P., Dey, E. L., Gurin, G., & Hurtado, S. (2003). How does racial diversity promote education? *Western Journal of Black Studies, 27*(1), 22–29.

Gurin, P., Dey, E. L., Hurtado, S., & Gurin, G. (2002, Fall). Diversity and higher education: Theory and impact on educational outcomes. *Harvard Educational Review, 72*(3), 330–366.

Hardy v. Jefferson Community College, 260 F.3d 671 (6th Cir. 2001).

Hazelwood School District v. Kuhlmeier, 484 U.S. 260 (1988).

Head v. Board of Trustees, 315 Fed. A'ppx 7 (9th Cir. 2008).

Head v. Board of Trustees, Civ. No. C 05-05328 WHA, 2006 WL 2355209 *1 (N.D. Cal. 2006).

Hutchens, N. H., & Sun, J. C. (2013). The tenuous legal status of First Amendment protection for individual academic freedom. *Journal of the Professoriate, 7*(1), 1–25.

Individuals with Disabilities Education Act, 20 U.S.C. § 1400 et seq. (2015).

Kaplan, D. M. (2014). Ethical implications of a critical legal case for the counseling profession Ward v. Wilbanks. *Journal of Counseling & Development*, 92(2), 142–146. doi:10.1002/j.1556-6676.2014.00140.x

Keeton v. Anderson-Wiley, 664 F. 3d 865 (11th Cir. 2011).

Lattuca, L.R. & Stark, J. S. (2009). *Shaping the college curriculum: Academic plans in context* (2nd edition). San Francisco: Jossey Bass.

Levin v. Harleston, 966 F.2d 85 (2d Cir. 1992).

Menand, L. (2019). The supreme court case that enshrined white supremacy in law. *New Yorker*. Retrieved from www.newyorker.com/magazine/2019/02/04/the-supreme-court-case-that-enshrined-white-supremacy-in-law

Milem, J. F., Chang, M. J., & Antonio, A. L. (2005). *Making diversity work on campus: A research-based perspective*. Washington, DC: Association American Colleges and Universities.

Oppenheimer, M. (2012, Feb. 4). A counselor's convictions put her profession on trial. *New York Times*, A18.

Oyama v. University of Hawaii, 813 F.3d 850 (9th Cir. 2015).

Pascarella, E. T., Salisbury, M. H., Martin, G. L., & Blaich, C. (2012). Some complexities in the effects of diversity experiences on orientation toward social/political activism and political views in the first year of college. *Journal of Higher Education*, 83(4), 467–496.

Regents of the University of Michigan v. Ewing, 474 U.S. 214 (1985).

Rudow, H. (2013). Resolution of EMU case confirms ACA Code of Ethics: Counseling profession's stance against client discrimination. *Counseling Today*. Retrieved from https://ct.counseling.org/2013/01/resolution-of-emu-case-confirms-aca-code-of-ethics-counseling-professions-stance-against-client-discrimination/

Sáenz, V. B., Ngai, H. N., & Hurtado, S. (2007). Factors influencing positive interactions across race for African American, Asian American, Latino, and White college students. *Research in Higher Education*, 48(1), 1–38.

Settle v. Dickson County School Board, 53 F.3d 152 (6th Cir. 1995).

Shaikh v. Lincoln Memorial University, 608 Fed. A'ppx. 349 (2015).

Stolzenberg, E. B., Eagan, M. K., Aragon, M. C., Cesar-Davis, N. M., Jacobo, S., Couch, V., & Rios-Aguilar, C. (2019). *The American freshman: National norms fall 2017* (expanded ed.). Los Angeles, CA: Higher Education Research Institute, UCLA.

Tatro v. University of Minnesota, 816 N.W.2d 509 (Minn. 2012).

Vasquez, M. (2019). The students called the TA a "Nazi": He said he's not a white supremacist. *Chronicle of Higher Education*. Retrieved from https://www.chronicle.com/article/The-Students-Called-the-TA-a/246133

Ward v. Polite, 667 F.3d 727 (6th Cir. 2012).

Chapter Three

Chapters and Verse
Free Speech, Inclusion, and Co-Curricular Experiences

The calls start coming into several administrative offices of the university as soon as their doors open that morning. Have they seen what is going on in the mall? Who authorized that? How do we get it stopped right now? What do we tell students who are unsettled, and in some instances frightened our nauseated, by what is taking place? Quickly checking the campus schedule for the day the Dean of Students sees that Saving Lives, a registered student organization, has reserved the mall for an event. The Dean gets to the mall to find a large semi-circle of very large, professionally developed billboard signs with graphic pictures of aborted fetuses, exterminated prisoners from Nazi concentration camps, Native American victims of governmental massacres, and people slaughtered in the Rwandan genocide. There are also billboards with large messages in texts arguing that abortion is genocide and that any support for genocide is immoral. Members of Saving Lives are present and engaged in active, in some instances heated, conversations with members of the campus community. Behind the students from the organization are a number of other people who are filming the entire event. The Dean later learns these are representatives of a national organization which produces these billboard events and is invited by student organizations to display them at colleges and universities. The Dean does not recall that the event request form from Saving Lives mentioned either the graphic nature of the exhibit or the involvement of an outside group in the event. While she takes all of this in, the Dean's attention is drawn to a scuffle on the edge of the exhibit. It appears that a student, whom the Dean recognizes as being a trans* person involved in a number of feminists campus organizations, is being grabbed by campus law enforcement. There is a giant piece of metal at their feet and a gaping hole in one of the billboards. Just as the Dean begins to move toward that scuffle, she looks around to see that the local media have arrived and are filming both the exhibit and the arrest. The Dean's cell phone is ringing, and email and text messages are pinging away. It is going to be a very, very long day.

One need not look very far or very hard to find evidence that discussion and disagreement about the intersection of espoused values of inclusion and free speech (as well as other First Amendment freedoms) and co-curricular college life are at the forefront of contemporary practice and policy in American higher education. This chapter visits that intersection through an exploration of contemporary events, legal cases and concepts, and lessons and recommendations for practice.

There are references throughout this chapter to First Amendment freedoms or rights afforded under the First Amendment. These terms are used for purposes of brevity to reference both those freedoms or rights extant at public colleges and universities as a matter of constitutional law and those freedoms and rights extended by private institutions to their students through various campus codes, policies, practices, and contracts.

The chapter begins by describing the relationship of the curriculum and co-curriculum in higher education before proceeding to discussion of a variety of ways in which questions about tensions between free speech and inclusion in co-curricular settings present themselves at colleges and universities in the contemporary context. We then move on to a review of key concepts and important cases related to First Amendment freedoms. While the balance of this review focuses on the closely related notions of freedom of speech and freedom of association, both freedom of religion and freedom of press are also addressed. That review is followed by presentation of some broad lessons to be taken from the key concepts and important cases which can inform the ways in which policies, practices, programs, and responses to situations can be planned and implemented in ways consistent with institutional values, including support for free speech and other First Amendment freedoms. Several specific recommendations are also offered for consideration. The chapter concludes with a brief look ahead to one particular question on the co-curricular horizon, inviting readers to reflect on the information shared in the chapter and how it might be helpful in addressing that question and others like it.

CURRICULUM AND CO-CURRICULUM

Student experiences, including learning and development, are shaped by both what goes on inside their college or university and outside of it. The internal activities, meaning those which are formally and legally functions of the college or university, may be understood as either curricular or co-curricular in nature.

Curricular activities are those directly associated with the specified academic functions of the institution—specific courses and classes; majors and minors leading to degrees; grading and advancement policies; and required internships or practicum are all examples of elements of the curriculum.

55

Co-curricular activities are those programs, practices, and services made available through the college or university to its students for the purpose of enhancing student learning and development and which are intended to augment and supplement the institution's curricular offerings. Student organizations, campus housing, intercollegiate athletics, and campus conduct codes and processes are all examples of co-curricular student life.

The line between external activities and internal activities is not always as simple as it seems. External activities may sometimes involve members of the university community acting outside of their institutional roles, but these events are not formally a part of the institution (for example, a group of people hanging out at an off-campus party might include a number of students). However, take that same activity with just a modification or two, and it is suddenly no longer outside the scope of institutional boundaries (for example, a student organization hosts a party off campus in order to avoid room rental fees or other restrictions at the student union). Responding to situations arising from either of these two parties may become a part of the co-curricular functions of a university. In the latter instance, the occasion is clearly a function of a university entity in as much as it is planned and presented by a student organization. In the former instance, were there to be harassment or threats by one student against another and if the institution's code of conduct for students asserts jurisdiction for such behaviors between students no matter where they take place, the subsequent handling of any student conduct case would become a part of the co-curriculum. Colleges and universities typically limit any jurisdictional claim to circumstances taking place outside of their direct control to only the most egregious of behaviors (harassment, intimidation, or violence) in as much as these behaviors may significantly impact on the ability of one or more students to pursue their educational opportunities.

CONTEMPORARY CONTEXT

That evidence can readily be discovered through reviewing events and situations taking place on college and university campuses across the country and in the data available about the experiences and views of students on our campuses. Not surprisingly, it can also be found in public discourse and political activity. This section will review some, but by no means all, of these types of evidence.

Events and Situations

Issues of First Amendment freedoms arise in a number of interesting and important ways across a broad array of co-curricular activities and programs. In this section we will revisit a sampling of examples which have taken place in recent years. As is often the case, these examples may touch on more than one of the five First Amendment freedoms.

One often repeated theme is that of incidents involving offensive speech related to various dimensions of human identity. A string of incidents involving various chapters of a single fraternal organization serves to illustrate this theme. A University of Oklahoma fraternity, riding a chartered bus to a chapter event in 2015, sang a song with lyrics indicating Blacks were not welcome as members of that organization and which alluded to the lynching of Blacks. Someone posted a video recording of that moment, and the video went viral. The chapter was closed by the national fraternal organization as a result (New, 2015a), though there was some evidence that the students' behavior on the bus reflected values institutionalized in the national body. It appeared the members at the University of Oklahoma learned the song at a national leadership event for the fraternity (New, 2015b). In addition, incidents like the one on the bus had taken place at other universities involving their local chapters of this particular national fraternal organization. The Washington University (St. Louis) chapter was suspended in 2013 following an incident in which some of its pledges spoke racial insults in the presence of other students of the institution who were Black (Toler, 2015). In December of 2014 the Clemson University chapter of the same national fraternity was placed on probation by that university after hosting a "Cripmas" party (Ohlheiser, 2015). The university severed its ties with the fraternal organization and expelled two students who were involved and led the racist song (Fernandez & Pérez-Peña, 2015). Take a moment to consider whether or not you believe the institution's decision was a correct one and what information is it that leads you to that belief?

As this manuscript is being written the issue of blackface on college campuses is once again in the news as a result of the resurfacing and reconsideration of pictures of various public figures from college yearbooks and other college photographs showing those individuals in blackface. These images are not merely historical artifacts of bygone behavior. There have been publicized incidents of individual students posting blackface images on social media at Tufts University and the University of Oklahoma in the past few years, and California Polytechnic University recently suspended fraternity and sorority activities after two instances in which racist photographs were posted online (Korn, 2019).

Sadly, we could go on and on citing instances of hateful speech in co-curricular settings targeting one group of students or another based on some aspect of their identity. These illustrations reflect patterns, potentially of organizational cultures with deep-seated tensions manifested into institutionalized biases.

By no means are First Amendment freedom situations arising in the co-curriculum limited to Greek Life. Another recent series of events at a university highlights the complexity of perspectives and positions which often are a part of these situations. A student at Texas State University wrote a column for the school paper in which he addressed his life experiences and perceptions about Whiteness and White privilege. He wrote, "I see white people as an aberration. . . . I hate you because you shouldn't exist. You are both the dominant apparatus and the voice in which all other cultures, upon meeting you, die" (Lanmon, 2017, pp. 1–6). The column sparked considerable reaction including a threat by the student body president to withdraw funding from the school paper, an effort to impeach the student body president, and a sit-in at the student center by students frustrated by what they saw as a failure on the part of the university president to address the death threats and hate mail to the student columnist with whose work she had publicly taken issue (Mangan, 2018b).

As the event at Texas State University demonstrates, the discussions and debates about First Amendment freedoms in co-curricular matters are sometimes about both speech and the reactions to it. The scheduling of speakers on campuses can lead to such situations. Students and others sometimes engage in efforts to protest the appearance of a particular speaker or to prevent a speaker from being heard. We have seen examples of this at Auburn University, Middlebury College, Texas Southern University, University of California at Berkeley, University of Florida, University of Wisconsin–Madison, and William and Mary (Adams, 2017; Andrews, 2017; Larimer, 2017), among others.

Some of these protest efforts may be seen as crossing over the line into conduct which is referred to as the heckler's veto where those protesting a speaker or event are seen as inhibiting free speech through their efforts to shout down the speaker or otherwise disrupt the event. A notable example took place at the University of Arizona in March of 2019 when the Criminal Justice Association, a recognized student organization, was hosting agents from United States Customs and Border Patrol who were speaking about career opportunities (Mangan, 2019b). Two students who were not members of the campus organization stood in the hallway outside the group's meeting and shouted that the Border Patrol agents murderers and likened them to the Ku Klux Klan. The students also reportedly followed the agents to their cars following the event. Both students were arrested and charged with a misdemeanor for interfering with the operation of a public institution, and one was charged with issuing threats and intimidation. In addition, the university indicated they would be reviewing whether the students' conduct violated its student code in any way. In an interesting turn of events indicative of how complex these situations can be, University of Arizona President Robert C. Robbins issued two statements on the incident indicating the institution values free speech but will not abide disruption of its activities. President Robbins noted in one of his statements that the University of Arizona was pleased to have a positive rating from the Foundation for Individual Rights in Education, an organization which advocates for free speech on college campuses. However, for its part, FIRE issued a statement noting that situations like the one at the University of Arizona require a difficult balance between competing free speech interests and that, typically, momentary instances of disruption which do not materially interfere with an event do not meet the test of disruption.

Tensions in co-curricular life may also center on tensions between First Amendment rights and multiple deeply held values within the campus community, including values related to institutional history, tradition, diversity, and inclusion. Such is the case with the ongoing activities on many campuses related to how an institution of higher education should conduct itself regarding historic monuments and named buildings or building features (whether named as a result of gifting or other action). While the issue of what to do with statues of foes vanquished by the United States is nothing new in our nation's history (Brock, Michelmore, & Horowitz, 2018), campus statuary, and in particular campus statues honoring persons associated with the Confederacy (especially those in states which were part of the Confederacy), have become a very public example of these tensions. Indeed, these situations are so plentiful that *The Chronicle of Higher Education* now tracks them (Bauman & Turnage, 2017). To be clear, the naming of a campus feature or the placement of a particular piece of statuary or art is not in and of itself a First Amendment issue. First Amendment issues may arise, however, out of the ways in which people engage and respond to those features, statues, or art pieces.

The marches by White nationalists in Charlottesville and at the University of Virginia, which were met by counter-protesters from campus and the community, were ostensibly organized (at least in part) to address plans to remove a statue from the area (Spencer & Stolberg, 2017). The ways in which those marches and counter-protests were handled by university and local authorities have been the subject of substantial post-event analysis and critique. The Silent Sam statue at the University of North Carolina in Chapel Hill (UNC) stood in a prominent location on that campus, and it was the center of considerable discussion, debate, and protest. At one point a UNC student put blood and red ink on the statue to contextualize the edifice from the perspective of those who saw it as a daily representation of slavery and the injustices to Blacks as a result of slavery (Patel, 2018). The student was charged with violations of the university's honor code, but those charges were later dismissed on procedural grounds (Associated

Press, 2019). Eventually a group of protestors on campus pulled the statue from its pedestal (Deconto & Blinder, 2018) which created a heightened sense of immediacy around what UNC should do with the statue. During those very public and contentious debates the chancellor decided to have the statue base removed from its location on campus. Many believe that this decision resulted in her early departure (she had already indicated her intention to step down at the end of her contract) from campus (Jacobs, 2019). More recently, White nationalists marched in Oxford, Mississippi and on the campus of the University of Mississippi to support, among other things, the presence of a statue at the University of Mississippi memorializing Confederate soldiers, and some members of the men's basketball team silently took a knee during the national anthem at a game on campus that evening (Aschoff, 2019). After a long, ongoing campus discussion of the question without resolution or action, students, staff, and faculty were seemingly catalyzed by the silent protests to move forward in votes recommending the relocation of the statue to a more suitable location in a nearby cemetery for fallen soldiers of the Confederacy (Rueb, 2019).

Student Perceptions and Opinions

Student perceptions and opinions regarding free speech and First Amendment rights also reflect the contested nature of these issues on our campuses. Information from two national surveys conducted by the Gallup organization and sponsored by the Knight Foundation (Gallup, 2018) on those perceptions and opinions is presented in this section of the chapter.

Students who responded to the survey published in 2018 reported a lesser sense of security regarding all five First Amendment rights (speech, religion, press, assembly, and right to petition government regarding grievances) than did their peers responding to a similar 2016 study (as cited in Gallup, 2018). The students responding to the most recent survey recognized both protecting free speech and promoting an inclusive society as important. However, when asked to pick which of those two propositions was the more important, 53% indicated promoting an inclusive society while 46% indicated protecting free speech. Students who identified as female, Black, and Democrat were more likely than their peers to select inclusive society.

It is interesting to note that in the same survey, when asked to pick between having a positive environment where certain kinds of speech would be prohibited and an open environment allowing offensive speech, 70% of the 2018 respondents selected the option of an open environment. Nearly two thirds of the students taking part in the study said they did not think hate speech, particularly slurs or speech intentionally offensive to groups, should be protected.

On the topic of specific technologies of protection, nearly 90% of the students favor spaces where students can go for support. Over 80% support establishing free speech zones, but a very slight majority resist the idea of speech codes or codes of conduct that restrict offensive or biased speech that would be permitted in society more broadly. Nearly three quarters oppose disinviting speakers because some students oppose those speakers, but nearly 70% favor canceling speeches if there are concerns about the possibility of violent protests. Ninety percent say violence in opposition to speakers is never acceptable whereas 62% say shouting down a speaker is never acceptable with 34% saying it is sometimes acceptable.

The students' thoughts on campus climate are also illuminating. Over 60% feel the climate on their campus prevents some people from saying things they believe because others find them offensive. Note that this is not to say whether the students see this as good or bad. A quarter of those taking part in the survey say they have felt uncomfortable as a result of something said on campus with this number being far higher for Black students (43%), particularly for those Black students enrolled at institutions other than Historically Black Colleges and Universities. Jewish students reported having felt uncomfortable as a result of something said more often than students from other religious groups, though it does not appear that results for Muslim students were included in the reporting of the data. While only 17% of students self-identified as Republicans said they had felt uncomfortable as a result so something said on campus, those same self-identified Republican students are significantly less likely than their peers to say that conservatives can express their views on campus (68% for Republicans versus 92% for Democrats or Independents).

The students participating in the study frequently had firmly held positions about free speech and First Amendment issues, but their knowledge about campus policies and practices in those areas was less in evidence. About 60% were unsure whether their college has a speech code or a free speech zone or whether their institution has disinvited a speaker. Over 60% are aware whether their campus makes safe spaces available for students.

Public Discourse and Political Activity

Student perceptions and opinions do not form in a vacuum. They reflect both internal learning and development as well as environmental presses, including the thoughts shared in public discourse and addressed through political activity.

American public support for First Amendment freedoms writ large remains strong. Support for free speech specifically has grown over the past several decades as evidenced in findings of the General Social Survey

(Yglesias, 2018). Among its questions, it asks respondents to indicate whether the five different types of speakers (communists, militarists, racists, homosexuals, and atheists) ought to be allowed to speak in their community if invited. Support for four of the five types of speakers has gone up since 1970 when the survey began. The only group for which it has remained relatively flat is for the racist speaker, but looking beyond the aggregate data provides a very helpful insight. Support for permitting the racist speaker has actually been flat for survey participants identifying themselves as moderate, slightly conservative, and conservative. Support has declined among those who are liberal and moderately liberal, but it has increased among both those who are extremely conservative and those who are extremely liberal (with the most marked increase among the former). This differentiation in the general public of opinion regarding free speech when it comes to matters of diversity and inclusion is not dissimilar to the differentiation we see in the responses of students when queried about their perceptions and opinions related to First Amendment freedoms. As a side note, about 20 years ago the General Social Survey added a question about whether an anti-American Muslim cleric ought to be allowed to speak. A majority of respondents across all political identifications indicate that cleric should not be permitted to appear.

Another national survey of adults in the United States also reveals support for free speech, specifically free speech on campus (Ciemnecki, 2018). It reports that 57% of adults say colleges should invite speakers to campus even if they have offended others. Here again, there is significant variation in response according to self-identified political affiliation. A majority of both Republicans (64%) and Independents (59%) support the proposition, but only 47% of Democrats concur. That same survey found 59% of those taking part in the survey think colleges lean one way or the other politically. Of those with that belief, 77% say colleges tend to be liberal whereas only 15% said colleges tend to be conservative. Nearly 80% of those who say that colleges lean one way or the other identify this as a problem, including nearly half who say it is a major problem.

These feelings on the part of the general public stand in stark contrast to the perceptions of college presidents, but in ways that indicate that, at least as an espoused value, college presidents (and by extension their institutions) are more supportive of free speech than the general public when it comes to exposing students to a variety of viewpoints even if those viewpoints may be offensive to some. Espinosa, Crandall, and Wilkinson (2018), reporting findings of a study conducted by the American Council on Education (ACE), note that nearly 100% of the presidents responding reported that both promoting an inclusive society that is welcoming to diverse groups and protecting citizens' free speech rights are extremely or very important in our democracy. While 20% of the presidents see campus inclusion goals and free speech goals as in conflict with one another, a similar overwhelming proportion (again, nearly 100%) said it is more important for colleges to allow students to be exposed to all types of speech even if they find it offensive or biased than it is to protect students by prohibiting speech they may find offensive or biased.

College presidents and their students have fairly similar thoughts when it comes to appropriate responses to controversial speakers. According to Espinosa, Crandall, and Wilkinson (2018), 85% of presidents say shouting down speakers is never acceptable (15% sometimes). Half say engaging in protest against speakers is always acceptable and 46% sometimes. A full 100% say using violence to stop a speech, protest, or rally is never acceptable. A majority of presidents say distributing literature on controversial issues is always acceptable with another 44% saying it is sometimes acceptable. Seventy percent of presidents say denying media access to cover a campus protest or rally is never acceptable. Somewhat surprisingly, 55% of college presidents say sit-ins or other attempts to disrupt campus operations are sometimes acceptable, and another 6% say they are always acceptable (though 38% say such actions are never acceptable). The notion of more speech as a way of addressing poor speech clearly resonates on the main with college presidents.

About half of presidents rate the students and faculty at their college as very good or good at seeking out and listening to viewpoints different than their own—notably higher than their perception of this quality for students and faculty at other colleges (Espinosa, Crandall, & Wilkinson, 2018). Nearly three quarters said the same of their staff and administrators (again, significantly higher than their assessment of staff and administrators at other colleges).

Though sanguine about the ways in which their faculty and staff colleagues value and receive diverse viewpoints, college presidents are concerned about the state of affairs on their campuses when it comes to managing efforts around inclusion and free speech (Espinosa, Crandall, & Wilkinson, 2018). A full 70% are either somewhat or very concerned about violence and student safety in this area. This concern is a bit surprising when considering that only 40% reported that students on their campuses have held demonstrations about issues of inclusion and diversity in the past year, 10% regarding free speech, and 9% against controversial speakers.

State legislatures have taken notice of public and student concerns regarding First Amendment issues on college campuses, particularly some from certain political and religious groups who feel their views are not represented or welcome on college campuses (see Adams, 2017; Kampis,

2018; Kurtz, Manley, & Butcher, 2017; Mangan, 2018a for example). These bills commonly affirm the importance of free speech on college campuses, prohibit institutions from doing anything to inhibit the exercise of free speech, prohibit free speech zones, and require colleges and universities to hold members of their community (particularly students) accountable for any infringements on free speech (Hutchens, 2017, 2019). It is not just state governments which are taking up free speech and First Amendment issues on college campuses. The Federal government is also engaging in this area, including the legislative branch (Larimer, 2017), executive agencies (Thomason, 2017), and the executive office itself (Mangan, 2019a). A more robust discussion of these and other external party influences is presented in Chapter 5.

KEY CONCEPTS AND IMPORTANT CASES

There is a great deal of contemporary activity related to First Amendment freedoms and American higher education, but there is nothing new about discussions related to First Amendment freedoms and co-curricular life on college campuses. Issues arose almost from the outset of the development of student organizations and the earliest vestiges of co-curricular life on campuses. One example took place at the University of Chicago in the early 1930s when students invited a leader of a communist party to speak on campus. In response to adverse reaction from the campus and community, President Robert Hutchins stood up for the right of students to hear diverse points of view as part of their education (Chemerinsky & Gillman, 2017).

Institutional policy and professional practice in the area of First Amendment freedoms, even at private institutions where such freedoms are provided through campus codes and other forms of contracts with students, have been shaped by considerations of legal decisions over this extended history. It can be helpful to be aware of and have some understanding of the strands in legal thinking about matters of the First Amendment and college co-curricular life as reflected in various court decisions. This section of the chapter will present an overview of that information, focusing on four of the five First Amendment freedoms: speech, assembly, religion, and press. The fifth, right to petition the government regarding grievances, is an area which has not seen much attention or activity as it relates to co-curricular life on college campuses.

Free Speech

There is little doubt based on long-standing legal precedent that the First Amendment right of free speech is present in the curricular and co-curricular life of students at public institutions of higher education as a matter of constitutional law, and freedoms fashioned after those provided for in the First Amendment are commonly extended to students at privately controlled colleges and universities as a matter of institutional policy and through various contracts between the student and the institution. *Tinker v. Des Moines Independent Community School District* (1969), which centers on public K-12 education, is the case which undergirds much of the controlling case law and legal thinking in this area.

There continues to be discussion and litigation surrounding the ways in which extant law related to co-curricular college life and free speech may be interpreted in light of the ever-changing but ubiquitous world of computer-mediated communication and social media. Much of that discussion, however, aligns itself with the idea laid out in *United States v. Alkhabaz aka Jake Baker* (1997) in which the court indicated computer-mediated communication might require some fine tuning of laws but does not change the basic analysis relative to the First Amendment (see Chapter 4 for an extended discussion of digital communication, inclusion, and free speech).

Of course, the issue of whether or not free speech rights are afforded to college students in their co-curricular endeavors is not a simple binary proposition. The answer for questions in this area, like the answer to so many good legal questions, is often, 'It depends.' Several of those contingencies are discussed below.

Exceptions

There are several forms of speech which are not protected as free speech. Those forms include fighting words, threats and intimidation, obscenity, defamation, and harassment (PEN America, 2017). The question presented at higher education institutions is not whether or not these particular types of utterances ought to be afforded protection; they should not. Instead, the question more often at hand is whether or not the particular words spoken can be considered as falling into one or more of these exceptions.

The origins of the *fighting words* doctrine as it is understood today derives from *Chaplinsky v. New Hampshire* (1942). Walter Chaplinsky was arrested for handing out pamphlets on a public sidewalk. Those pamphlets described a particular city official as a "God-damned racketeer and a damned Fascist." His conviction was upheld as the court found that words such as these are likely to provoke a violent response or to grievous emotional injury. The decision was later narrowed in *Cohen v. California* (1971) where it was found that the California statute underlying the conviction of Paul Cohen, who was charged for wearing a clothing with "Fuck the draft. Stop the war." printed on it, was overly broad. Fighting words must be directed at a person and likely to provoke a physical action. The fighting words principle was also more clearly defined through the decision in *R.A.V. v. City of St. Paul* (1992). Teenagers had been convicted of a crime for burning a cross on the lawn of a Black family. While the behavior was clearly repugnant, the court found that the underlying law only addressed language addressed toward some protected classes of people and held that the state cannot prohibit some fighting words and not others. In a subsequent case, *Virginia v. Black* (2003), three men were found guilty of intent to intimidate for burning a cross in a field in Virginia, but the court overturned their conviction and noted that sometimes cross burning can be symbolic and sometimes it can be fighting words or a true threat (see below for more on true threats). In this case, given the location of the behavior, the court found the cross burning could be symbolic speech. However, it is important to note that there is no recent higher education legal case in which speech has been found by a court to constitute fighting words as imagined in the doctrine.

The *Virginia v. Black* (2003) case defines a *true threat* as reflecting the intent of the person speaking to express a serious intent to commit violence against an individual or group of individuals, including such expressions for the purpose of intimidation. That definition follows in the tradition of decisions which focus on whether or not the expression in question is clear, direct, and serious in intent. In *Watts v. United States* (1969), the court found that Robert Watts' statement that, if drafted, his first gun target would be President Lyndon Johnson was political hyperbole rather than a genuine literal statement. This stands in contrast to the decision in *United States v. Kelner* (1976). Here the court found that Russell Kelner's comments about plans to assassinate Yasser Arafat during a visit to New York were indicative of serious and specific intent. In another important case, *Planned Parenthood of Columbia/Willamette, Inc., et al. v. American Coalition of Life Advocates, et al.* (2002), the AACLA group created a web site with 'wanted posters' identifying health care professionals providing abortion services and indicating they could be held accountable at future war crimes trials. The web site also listed information about abortion service providers and noted when they were injured or killed because they provided those services. The court observed that advocating violence is protected speech, but threatening a person with violence is not. The wanted posters alone were not sufficient evidence of a true threat, but when taken in consideration with the listing of those injured or murdered the AACLA's speech could reasonably be understood as a threat.

The courts do not offer much in the way of specific guidance when it comes to what constitutes *obscenity*. Supreme Court Justice Potter Stewart, in offering a definition of pornography in *Jacobellis v. Ohio* (1964), famously observed that he would know it when he saw it. The decision in *Miller v. California* (1973) provides a more substantial, though still challenging, set of criteria in deciding that obscenity must depict or describe sexual conduct as specifically defined in applicable law and must, when taken on the whole, appeal to prurient sexual interest; portray sexual conduct in a patently offensive way; and (again, when taken on the whole) have no serious literary, artistic, political, or scientific value. Most important for those considering such matters in terms of the co-curricular life of students in colleges and universities, *Papish v. Board of Curators of the University of Missouri* (1973) is crystal clear with regard to the applicability of free speech on students writing about matters of public concern on public campuses.

Unlike as with obscenity, the courts have offered a fairly succinct definition of *defamation*.

> Common law and constitutional doctrines require that (1) the statement be false; (2) the publication serve to identify the particular person libeled; (3) the publication cause at least nominal injury to the person libeled; usually including but not limited to injury to reputation; and (4) the falsehood be attributed to some fault on the part of the person or organization publishing it.
>
> (Kaplin & Lee, 2013, p. 1320)

The identity of the person alleging injury helps define the degree of fault required for speech to be considered as defamation. If the person is a public figure, the standard is that it must be made with knowledge that it is false or with reckless disregard for whether it is true or false. If a person is other than a public figure, then the standard is simply that of negligence (Kaplin & Lee, 2013). An important consideration for colleges and universities in the area of defamation is the question of whether or not the institution is responsible for statements made in student publications. Greater liability comes when a college or university sponsors the publication, the editorial staff is employed by the institution, and when the institution exercises some form of formal advanced review of content prior to publication (Kaplin & Lee, 2013).

Harassment is another form of speech which is not protected by the First Amendment, but as we have seen with other exempted categories of speech, the trick is in coming to an understanding of what constitutes harassment and being sure that in addressing harassing behavior we do not infringe on otherwise protected speech. The legal definition of harassment varies by states, but those definitions generally describe unwelcomed, unwanted, and uninvited conduct (including speech) which is annoying, threatening, or intimidating ("Harassment law and legal definition, 2016). Higher education institutions which engage in policies or practices to prevent or address harassing behavior in a broad sense are generally on solid ground. However, when in an effort to advance their institutional values of inclusion and respect these policies or practices begin to take the form of speech codes then they may run far greater risk of being seen by the courts as interfering with protected speech.

Speech Codes

As colleges and universities have sought to advance their institutional interests in diverse, inclusive, and respectful campus communities, they have looked to include language in their student codes of conduct related to speech which may be considered hostile or offensive (Beassie & Gomez, 2015). These efforts, sometimes referred to as speech codes, typically are intended to address what is commonly referred to as hate speech—a term for which there is no meaningful legal construct (Chemerinsky & Gillman, 2017; Kaplin & Lee, 2013). Successful challenges to campus speech codes have been made on the basis that they are overly broad and interfere with protected speech (see either Doe v. University of Michigan (1989) or UWM Post, Inc., v. Board of Regents of the University of Wisconsin System (1991), for example).

Forums

One final and critically important element in consideration of freedom of speech on college campuses is the forum—where the speech takes place. Broadly speaking, the law recognizes three types of forums at higher education institutions: *public, limited public,* and *private or non-forum* (Lake, 2011). The more open the forum, the more free the speech. Peter Lake rightfully and wisely advises,

> The mantra of wide viewpoint access and reasonable regulation in light of the purposes of a forum should perpetually reverberate in . . . practice. The actual process of illuminating the educational and developmental nature and purposes of a forum is critical in any legal challenge to regulations under the First Amendment.
>
> (2011, p. 213)

"A traditional public forum is a neutral field . . . as long as the speech is protected speech, these spaces are free from content/viewpoint censorship. They include public thoroughfares and green spaces that are traditionally open to the public, such as parks" (Lake, 2011, p. 208). According to Kaplin and Lee (2006),

> Since the right of access is based on the First Amendment, and since the property involved must be government property, public forum issues generally arise only at public colleges and universities. Such issues could become pertinent to a private college or university, however, if its students were engaging, or planning to engage, in speech activities on public streets or sidewalks that cut through or are adjacent to the private institution's campus; or if its students were using other government property in the vicinity of the campus for expressive purposes.
>
> (p. 997)

Reasonable time, place, and manner restrictions are possible for public forums.

A limited public forum is one created by an institution of higher education. In the act of creation, the institution imbues a limited public forum with certain qualities that make it different from other fora. . . . Limited public fora include systems of student publications, registered student organizations (RSOs), student activity systems, some Internet functions, and certain billboards.

> (Lake, 2011, p. 211)

Limited public forums are also sometimes referred to a designated forums (Kaplin & Lee, 2006). Viewpoint discrimination is not permissible in limited public forums, but content can be regulated if reasonable in light of the established purpose for the forum.

In a variation on the commonly understood notion of a limited public forum, "some fora are not open to the public generally but are open only for a very select purpose. An institution of higher education can permit "selective access for individual speakers rather than general access for a class of speakers." These fora are subject to a slightly lower standard of scrutiny than limited public fora" (Lake, 2011, p. 217).

Finally,

> Some spaces are not fora at all. Some fora are not open to the public generally; some are not even open for speech. In such places, the freedom of speech/association of the institution of higher education itself (or the student affairs administrator or other employee) may be at stake, and allowing forum analysis would squelch speech or association and/or the dedicated use of the property for a non-speech purpose.
>
> (Lake, 2011, p. 218)

69

Forum analysis is not for the ill-informed or faint-of-heart. There are a variety of variables which may be at play when considering what type of forum is at hand, and those variables may shift depending on who the various participants are in the situation at hand and the purpose for which the speech is being undertaken. Any serious discussion of the creation of new forums, development or revision of regulations for extant forums, or response to concerns or disagreements about how speech will or has played out in a forum really ought to include the advice of counsel (and perhaps consultation with outside counsel).

Time, Place, and Manner

Even when speech is protected by First Amendment freedoms or their equivalent in private college settings, institutions of higher education can take reasonable steps to regulate the time, place, and manner of that speech. Any effort to regulate speech ought to be developed keeping in mind a four-prong test through which courts have consistently evaluated challenges to time, place, and manner restrictions (see Grayned v. City of Rockford (1972) or Clark v. Community for Creative Non-Violence (1984), for example). First, does the regulation serve an important institutional interest that would be less effectively achieved were the regulation not in place (Lake, 2011)? Second, is the regulation content neutral (neither hindering nor advancing a particular viewpoint and applied consistently regardless of content of the speech)? While the regulation has to be content neutral, it is nonetheless permissible that it might impact some speakers more than others (Lake, 2011). Third, is the regulation constructed narrowly while meeting the important institutional interest? The regulation does not have to be the least restrictive option available, but it must not be overly broad in ways which could inhibit otherwise permissible speech (Lake, 2011). Fourth and finally, do ample alternatives remain open for conveying the message(s)?

As part of their policies and practices related to establishing time, place, and manner restrictions, many colleges and universities have processes through which student organizations and other campus entities are required to go in order to have their events approved. *Bayless v. Martine* (1970) and other cases offer plentiful support for such processes. However, as noted above, any element of a prior approval process that makes inquiry as to the content of the program invites the opportunity for the appearance of a decision-making process which inappropriately considers content. It is fine to ask if the event is a speaker, performance, band, demonstrations, or other form of activity. It is unwise to ask what the speech, performance, concert, demonstration, or other activity will be about.

70

One not uncommon outcome of the filing of an event registration form is that a college or university may become concerned about additional costs. Higher education institutions may charge reasonable fees to cover the additional costs associated with events being held on campus. Such a fee does not constitute an infringement on First Amendment freedoms if based on the type of event and not the content. A campus might say that events that are expected to draw less than X people will not be charged any additional fee. Events expected to draw X number of people to a venue will be charged a fee of Y to help cover costs associated with additional personnel for traffic control and cleaning. Events of X + Z people will be charged Y + W for those services. The following example illustrates this model. Grand Old Fictional University (GOFU), a small private institution with policies assuring students of free speech very similar to those afforded through the First Amendment as well as a robust academic freedom policy, has an event fee policy which is intended to balance the university's interest in offering an active and vibrant intellectual and social life on campus with the budgetary realities of being a smaller institution with modest operating financial resources. Hence, GOFU's event service fee policy for campus departments or organizations (including RSOs) provides for fixed and tiered event service fees based on anticipated attendance, duration of the event, and time of day. The event service fee helps defray security and custodial costs. It is charged in addition to any applicable facility rental fee or equipment and technical support fee. There is no event service fee charged for events with anticipated attendance of 100 or fewer persons which last for four hours or less and which occur between 7am and 10pm (standard operating hours). Events with an anticipated attendance of 100 or fewer which are expected to last more than four hours during standard operating hours are charged $20 per hour for each additional hour, and events of a similar size occurring outside standard operating hours are charged $45 for all hours of service. Events with an anticipated attendance of 101–500 people during standard operating hours are charged $45 per hour for all hours of the event, and similar events hosted outside standard operating hours are charged $67.50 per hour. Events of 501–1,000 people during standard operating hours are charged $90 per hour for all hours of the event, and similar events hosted outside standard operating hours are charged $135 per hour. GOFU does not schedule events where attendance is anticipated to be more than 1,000 people as it does not have facilities which can safely accommodate that many folks.

Colleges and universities may not say that events will be charged nothing, Y, or Y + W depending on the content of the event or the nature of the people likely to attend (see College Republicans of University of Washington v. Cauce, 2018 for example). Consideration of event fee policies is not only an important matter of law; it is also relevant to both higher education's mission of education and its espoused value of inclusion. Arbitrary and inhibitive fees may prevent some perspectives from being heard and some communities from being represented in scholarly and artistic life of campus. It should also be noted that the *Cauce* case centered on a claim related to an institutional policy requiring reimbursement of expenses. If the expenses for which an institution is requesting reimbursement are variable in any way that could be open to allegations of content bias, reimbursement policies and practices can be just as problematic as up-front fees with similar vulnerabilities.

Some campuses, in their effort to advance what they see as reasonable time, place, and manner restrictions, may be attracted to designating certain parts of their campuses as areas for free speech activities—so called *free speech zones*. While an understandable inclination in some ways, efforts such as these are fraught with legal peril given the test articulated by the courts for evaluating the reasonableness of such restrictions (Lake, 2011).

> Free speech zones will raise serious difficulties under these requirements [U.S. Supreme Court's public forum cases, including three-part test of *Clark v. Community for Creative Non-Violence*] in at least two circumstances. First, if the institution's regulations allow free speech only in the approved zone or zones, and if other parts of the campus that are unavailable for speech activities are considered traditional public forums, serious issues will arise because traditional public forum property cannot be entirely closed off to expressive uses. Second, if some but not all of the other campus areas that are public forums (besides the free speech zones) are left open for some or all expressive activity, other serious issues may arise under the *Clark/Ward* three part test.
>
> (Kaplin & Lee, 2006, p. 1006)

Heckler's Veto

Colleges and universities sometimes are faced with requests for events, programs, or protests which they believe may result in significant disruption or violence. However, a determination about whether or not to allow the event, program, or protest generally should not be premised on such a belief. Allowing the threat of interruption to prohibit speech is commonly referred to as a heckler's veto, and the courts have been very clear on this point. "The mere possibility of a violent reaction to . . . speech is . . . not a constitutional basis on which to restrict the right to speech. . . . The First Amendment knows no heckler's veto" (Lewis v. Wilson, pp. 1077,

1081–1082). In addition, when responding to disruption of a university activity by students, the institution is well-advised to keep in mind the finding from *Shamloo v. Mississippi State Board of Trustees* (1980) that the standard is material and substantial disruption and not just episodic and annoying impeding.

Examples of Application of the Law

It may be helpful to offer a more extended review of several cases revolving around campus' efforts to balance their interests in both free speech and inclusion. These examples offer insight into the lines of reason discussed in this section of the chapter.

Offensive Expression

One line of court cases tackled the offensive expressions of already marginalized groups on campus via co-curricular events (see, e.g., Bair v. Shippensburg University, 2003; Doe v. University of Michigan 1989; Iota Xi Chapter of Sigma Chi Fraternity v. George Mason University, 1993). In these cases, a group of college students advanced a climate that mocked role incongruity through behavioral stereotyping, group humiliation, and inter-group bias.

Iota XI Chapter of Sigma Chi Fraternity v. George Mason University (1993) illustrates the prototypical expressions and behaviors emergent in these cases, and it also demonstrates how coercive isomorphism and legal consciousness only frame the matter and resolution in a limited manner because it fails to appreciate an adequate policy level. A fraternity hosted an annual week-long event of competitions among the university's Greek community. One event included an 'ugly woman contest' that fostered demeaning portrayals of women. As part of the contest, men "dressed as caricatures of different types of women, including one member dressed as an offensive caricature of a black woman" (p. 388). Specifically, "[h]e was painted black and wore stringy, black hair decorated with curlers, and his outfit was stuffed with pillows to exaggerate a woman's breasts and buttocks. He spoke in slang to parody African-Americans" (p. 388). The university imposed several sanctions on the fraternity chapter including a suspension for the rest of the academic year, a two-year prohibition on social activities other than pre-approved events such as philanthropic events, educational components about gender and cultural diversity, and a required plan to address cultural and gender inclusion. Analyzing various constitutional protections under the First Amendment, the federal appellate court related the skit to the law determined around constitutional rights of entertainment. Citing *Ward v. Rock against Racism* (1989), a Supreme Court case, the court stated it has become well established that music is a form of expression and communication that is generally protected under the First Amendment. Similarly, motion pictures and dance offer valued expressions, which are also protected under the First Amendment. Classifying the skit as entertainment, albeit low-grade entertainment, the federal court concluded that the skit was inherently expressive and subject to constitutional protections. Indeed, "[i]t may be that the performances were crude and amateurish and perhaps unappealing, but the same thing can be said about many theatrical performances," but so long as the expression in the form of a performance does not qualify as under the narrowly defined standards of obscenity, defamatory, true threat, or other impermissible expressions, then the First Amendment protections apply (Schacht v. United States, 1980 as cited in Iota Xi Chapter, 1993, 390). The *Iota Xi Chapter* case clarified that the First Amendment does not limit its protection based on quality of the performance.

By contrast, in *UWM Post, Inc. v. Board of Regents* (1991), the University of Wisconsin System's 26 campuses adopted a 'Design for Diversity' plan which guided the development or modification of policies, including student conduct policies, to advance non-discriminatory behaviors. The plan was adopted in response to highly publicized events at the Madison campus. Three incidents caught the attention of administrators. For one event, a fraternity "erected a large caricature of a black Fiji Islander" as part of its party theme (UWM Post, Inc. v. Board of Regents, 1991, p. 1165). Later that year, members from two fraternities were involved in a fight based on racial overtones. A year later, a fraternity "held a 'slave auction' at which pledges in black face performed skits parroting black entertainers" (UWM Post, Inc. v. Board of Regents, 1991, p. 1165). Three law professors at the University of Wisconsin–Madison assisted with the student conduct, nondiscrimination policy. Following the adoption of the policy, a series of behaviors across multiple Wisconsin campuses led to discipline under this policy—primarily for racial and sexual epithets. The court concluded that the phrase "discriminatory comments, epithets or other expressive behavior," as applied in the university system's rule of prohibiting students from directing discriminatory comments, epithets and other expressive behavior at particular individuals with intent to demean them and create hostile educational environment was constitutionally permissible (UWM Post, Inc. v. Board of Regents, 1991, p. 1179). Drawing on sources including the dictionary definitions of key terms used in the code, the federal court observed that words and phrase were clear and valid.

What accounts for the differing outcome in the two cases? George Mason did not rely on a specific policy in its argument, and it had relevant policy upon which to rely. The University of Wisconsin–Madison, however, took action pursuant to a clearly defined policy for "discriminatory comments, epithets or other expressive behavior" that was targeted at particular individuals with "intent to demean" them "and create hostile educational environment." These phrases reached further into the policy domain and repositioned the fulcrum to focus on the legally permissible conduct for which the First Amendment does not protect, and the focused language furthers the equity and social justice values of the university.

Provocative Expression

In one line of court cases, the controversy revolved around intentionally provocative expressions to capture the audience's attention and create dialogue (see, e.g., Abbott v. Pastides, 2018; College Republicans at San Francisco State v. Reed, 2007; Rock for Life-UMBC v. Hrabowski, 2010; UWM Post, Inc. v. Board of Regents, 1991). In these cases, a group of college students typically sought to display or convey messages that violated social norms or created an emotive reaction to spur debate and test the limits of the audience through co-curricular campus settings.

In *College Republicans at San Francisco State v. Reed* (2007), students participated in an 'Anti-Terrorism Rally' at San Francisco State University (SFSU). The university received several reports that some members of the College Republicans "very evidently walked over and trekked over a banner with Arabic script . . . [representing] the word 'Allah,' otherwise known as the name of God in Arabic" (p. 1008). The SFSU Director of the Office of Student Programs and Leadership Development conducted an investigation and referred the case to the Student Organization Hearing Panel so the formal conduct review board would hear the case. After witness testimony and review of the conduct violation allegations, the hearing panel concluded that the College Republicans had not violated the code. Nonetheless, the College Republicans filed suit against the university claiming that the student conduct policies were overbroad and vague. The student conduct code included a provision that held students responsible "to be civil to one another and to others in the campus community" with penalties associated with such violations. The federal court hearing the case concluded that the student conduct code was unconstitutionally overbroad in its reach because, as written, the university's policy covered expressions and activities that were otherwise permissible. Explaining the concept of an impermissibly overbroad policy, the court described:

> One way to conceptualize this task is to envision two spheres, one inside the other. Both spheres contain activity that reasonable

75

people would understand is subject to control by the regulation that is being examined to determine if it is overbroad. The outer, larger sphere contains (captures) all of the activity that falls within the reasonably construed reach of the regulation. In contrast, the inner, smaller sphere, contains only some of the activity that falls within the reach of the regulation; what sets the inner sphere apart is that it contains only activity that it is perfectly lawful for the government to restrict or burden through the kind of regulation that is being challenged. So all the speech or conduct that falls within the inner sphere is speech or conduct that the Constitution permits the government to regulate. The speech or expressive conduct that falls within the outer, larger sphere, but that is not within the inner sphere, is the speech or conduct that is covered by the challenged regulation but that the First Amendment prohibits the government from restricting or burdening. After determining the size of each of these two spheres, we compare them. If the inner sphere takes up most of the space within the outer sphere, the regulation is not overbroad. But if the outer sphere is substantially larger than the inner sphere, the law is overbroad in violation of the First Amendment and must be stricken.

(College Republicans, 2007, pp. 1013–1014)

In short, a sanction for not being civil to each other avails great possibility for a student to be disciplined for expressions protected under the First Amendment.

By contrast, in *Abbott v. Pastides* (2018), two student groups, the College Libertarians and Young Americans for Liberty, hosted a 'Free Speech Event' at the University of South Carolina to educate students about the various threats on free speech at college campuses. As part of the event, the student groups indicated that they would create mock symbols and present speeches that have been censored in other settings. Among the group's posters there was "one depicting a large red swastika and another featuring the word 'wetback' in outsized print" (Abbott v. Pastides, 2018, p. 165). The event generated several complaints based on racial and sexual harassment so the university's Equal Opportunity Programs Office investigated the matter. The preliminary inquiry was part of the pre-compliant process to determine if there should be a full investigation and notice of official charges alleged against the student groups. These insensitive expressions occurred on a campus with serious concerns about climate and culture with racial inclusion. In 2010, the U.S. Department of Justice entered into an agreement with the University of South Carolina based on complaints about racial discrimination and harassment on its campus.

Thus, the concern was very real for members of this campus. The preliminary inquiry concluded no cause for an investigation, and the matter was dissolved. Nonetheless, the student leaders sued the university alleging that the inquiry had a chilling effect on free speech and violated the First Amendment. A trial court ruled that the inquiry is an acceptable standard practice which did not constitute a disciplinary review. Further, because there were no threats of penalty, the actions did not have a chilling effect. While the expressions in this case would likely be deemed offensive and hurtful, the university's Director of Campus Life respected the parameters of the First Amendment and, when approving the event, she concluded that there was "no controversy in educating [the] campus about what is happening in the world" around democracy with open opportunities to express political messages (Abbott v. Pastides, 2018, p. 165). According to the case, "she hoped the event would be 'a chance to learn and grow (and even be a bit uncomfortable), not further any intolerance, censorship or acts of incivility'" (Abbott v. Pastides, 2018, p. 165).

Here again, what is the difference between these seemingly similar cases with very different outcomes? In the San Francisco State University case, the reference to being civil was part of the general goal and was properly placed in a policy location similar to a policy preamble, not as an enforceable policy with sanctions associated with it. Nonetheless, San Francisco State University wrote in its notification of wrongdoing letter to the students a reference about incivility as a violation and associated with sanctions. That civility inclusion as both an expressed violation with sanctions was impermissible because the mandate of civility potentially penalizes students for expressions that would also fall within their constitutionally protected free speech rights. Accordingly, the court declared the policy as unconstitutionally overbroad. The University of South Carolina case was much more straight-forward. There were no penalties. There was, however, an inquiry into the complaints. The University of South Carolina respected the free speech rights of the student groups without endorsing the expressions and treating the event as an education opportunity of differing perspectives.

Freedom of Association

Freedom of speech and freedom of association are closely related, and the courts have protected both when it comes to the co-curricular life of students at colleges and universities (Lake, 2011). As is the case with speech, institutions of higher education may require that groups of students wishing to be afforded the full privileges of institutional recognition register with the university. Colleges can require proof of student interest; a constitution describing the purpose of the organization; eligibility for membership and responsibility of members, process for selecting officers and their responsibilities; process for removing or replacing members or officers; and process for revising the constitution; regular updates on officers; and signed statements from officers acknowledging their responsibility to assure the organization complies with institutional rules and regulations. Groups successfully completing the process become Registered (or Recognized) Student Organizations (RSOs).

It is not uncommon that colleges and universities have several pathways through which a group can become an RSO, including the student government for general campus groups, campus religious offices for faith-based organizations, athletic and recreation departments for club sports, and deans or department chairs for academic organizations. Regardless of the pathway, it is very important that the recognition process be clearly articulated and consistently adhered to across all areas of the institution in ways which do not interfere with freedom of association or other First Amendment freedoms.

Two important cases clearly lay out the position of the courts with regard to RSO consideration. First, in *Healy v. James* (1972), a case in which Connecticut State College denied student organization recognition to a local chapter of Students for a Democratic Society because chapters on other campuses had been associated with disruption and violence, the ruling made it clear that colleges and universities cannot engaging in prior restraint in denying recognition merely on the basis of concern that a particular group will engage in problematic behavior. Instead, institutions can require that group officers sign a statement saying that they and the group will abide by institution rules and then pursue the matter if the group breaks its word. Second, in *Christian Legal Society v. Martinez* (2010), which centered on the rights of a faith-based organization to deny membership to persons not professing the faith, the Supreme Court described RSOs as a limited public forum, noted the importance that they can play in student learning as part of co-curricular life, and therefore noted the courts should generally defer to the judgment of higher education institutions when deciding on matters of First Amendment Freedoms and RSOs. Justice Stevens, in his concurring opinion (pp. 4–5), wrote:

> Academic administrators routinely employ anti-discrimination rules to promote tolerance, understanding, and respect, and to safeguard students from individuous forms of discrimination. Applied to the RSO [Recognized Student Organization] context, these values can, in turn, advance numerous pedagogical objectives. . . . The campus is, in fact, a world apart from the public square in numerous respects, and religious organizations, as well as all other organizations, must

abide by certain norms of conduct when they enter an academic community. . . . As a general matter, courts should respect universities' judgements and let them manage their own affairs.

Higher education institutions should also assure that any campus entity which has the authority to recognize an RSO and any campus entity that has the authority to sanction an RSO (for example, the dean of students office) has clearly articulated policies and practices for such action which are consistent with First Amendment freedoms, due process requirements, and other legal obligations.

The First Amendment right to associate also infers a right not to associate. This idea has been the source of litigation as well, principally as it relates to the collection and allocation of student fees (Kaplin & Lee, 2013). *Good v. Associated Students of the Univ. of Washington* (1975) and *Board of Regents of University of Wisconsin System v. Southworth* (2000), when taken together, are helpful in elucidating current legal thinking in this area. Colleges and universities may not require that students are members of a student government (or any student organization), but they may assess mandatory student fees which are in turn allocated (either directly by the institution or through the student government or other mechanism) to student organizations as long as the allocation of those fees remains viewpoint neutral (Kaplin & Lee, 2013).

Freedom of Religion

The Establishment Clause of the Constitution "prohibits the government from establishing an official religion, but also prohibits government actions that unduly favor one religion over another. It also prohibits the government from unduly preferring religion over non-religion, or non-religion over religion" (Legal Information Institute, n.d., 1). In *Lemon v. Kurtzman* (1971), the court identified a three-part test for determining whether or not a particular government action is consistent with the Establishment Clause. Does the action have a secular purpose? Does the action have a primary effect that neither advances nor inhibits religion? Does the action avoid producing excessive government entanglement? The *Lemon* test served to inform two important cases related to freedom of religion in students' co-curricular life on campus. The court ruling in *Widmar v. Vincent* (1981) struck down a rule preventing use of university facilities for religious teaching or worship, and *Christian Legal Society v. Martinez* (2010) found that the all comers policy (all students being welcome to join all RSOs) at the University of California at Hastings College of Law was content neutral and therefore neither promoted nor inhibited religion.

79

Freedom of the Press

Papish v. Board of Curators of the University of Missouri (1973), which was discussed in Chapter 1, is an important case with regard to the right of free press when it comes to student media. The court held that student publications have the same First Amendment protections that are afforded to the general media. As a practical matter, this includes freedom from prior restraint or censorship (Kaplin & Lee, 2013).

Advertising in student publications, however, is considered commercial speech and as such is not afforded the same protections. *Central Hudson Gas & Electric Corp. v. Public Service Commission of New York* (1980) puts forth a four-part test in determining whether or not speech is commercial. Does it concern an unlawful act, or is it misleading? Is the government interest at hand substantial? Does the regulation directly advance that governmental interest? Is the regulation narrowly tailored to serve that interest? Student publications may, for a variety of reasons, wish to carry advertisements related to activities that the university believes should not be promoted on campus—nude dancing, tobacco, or alcohol for example. There is no consensus in court opinions as to whether or not colleges and universities are on solid legal ground in attempting to assert policies which prohibit student publications from accepting such advertising (Kaplin & Lee, 2013).

Another important source of guidance regarding freedom of the press on college campuses is *OSU Student Alliance v. Ray* (2012). The OSU Student Alliance, an RSO at Oregon State University, had distributed *The Liberty* (their conservative newspaper) in bins across campus with permission from the institution. Suddenly and without notice, the bins and copies of the newspaper were removed from campus by university employees. The explanation was that the institution was now enforcing an extant policy relative to decluttering campus. Upon review, it turned out there was no written policy in this matter and that the bins of other papers continued to be available on campus. OSU Student Alliance requested permission to return their bins to campus, and they were granted approval to do so on a highly limited basis in designated areas. The court found that the university's action constituted a violation of the First Amendment in that the action it has taken was not content neutral, was previously unannounced, and was inconsistently enforced.

BROAD LESSONS

Drawing upon the key concepts and important cases we have just discussed, this section presents a number of broad lessens for consideration by those engaged in supporting the co-curricular life of students on campus and interested in assuring that their efforts in that regard are respectful and supportive of free speech and other First Amendment freedoms associated with that valuable aspect of the student experience.

If it was not already the case before beginning this chapter, it should be clear now that the courts have clearly and consistently found students at public institutions maintain First Amendment protections in co-curricular endeavors and settings as a matter of constitutional law and students at private institutions commonly have similar protections afforded to them as a matter of the policies and practices of their colleges and universities as well as their contracts with those colleges. The principle of the presence of these freedoms is steadfast; the interpretation and application of the law relative to these freedoms is more variable, though changes tend to come about through slow evolution rather than in lurching and erratic fashion. The first broad lesson of the chapter is this relative constancy in the law can serve as a reliable construct to inform to institutional policies, programs, and responses to situations on campus.

This brings us to the second broad lesson of the chapter. The closer the activity, policy, or program is to the core higher education function of the institution the greater the deference the court is likely to show to the institution (Lake, 2009; Sun, Hutchens, & Breslin, 2013).

> Colleges are primarily designed to be educational institutions. The Supreme Court has consistently and vigorously protected core mission delivery and made it clear that speech rights must nod to the college's right to deliver core mission without substantial and material disruption.
>
> (Lake, 2011, p. 201)

Extending from the second lesson, the third broad lesson of the chapter is that the courts do see the value of co-curricular life in student learning and development which is viewed as the core function of higher education. Supreme Court Justice Kennedy observed in his concurring opinion in *Christian Legal Society v. Martinez* (2010),

> Many educational institutions . . . have recognized that the process of learning occurs both formally in a classroom setting and informally outside of it. Students may be shaped as profoundly by their peers as by their teachers. Extracurricular activities . . . facilitate interactions between students, enabling them to explore new points of view, to develop talents and interests, and to nurture a growing sense of self.
>
> (p. 3)

81

Hence, the greater the extent to which a college or university can demonstrate a purposeful, thoughtful, and consistent connection between its co-curricular and curricular offerings the greater the likelihood that its position will prevail in any legal disagreement centered on First Amendment freedoms.

The fourth broad lesson from this chapter is an echo of an established truism when it comes to free speech.

> The reach of the First Amendment is broad, and often exceedingly distasteful or unpopular speech must be tolerated. Much that is hateful, rude, and repulsive has constitutional protection. The typical remedy for bad speech is more speech, not rules and punishment. (pp. 198–199)

Put another way, when your first inclination in developing policies, programs, or response to an emerging situation related to co-curricular life is to narrow options or opportunities for speech (or other First Amendment freedoms), pause, reflect, and reconsider.

RECOMMENDATIONS

We also offer the following more specific recommendations to those playing a role on their campuses in advancing inclusion while also supporting free speech and other First Amendment freedoms on campus. In doing so, we are mindful that the specific mechanisms used to employ these recommendations and the precise shape they will take on any given campus will vary based on the unique circumstances of that college or university.

Several of our recommendations relate to steps that can be taken before a situation arises on campus. To be clear, taking these steps will not prevent such situations from occurring. They almost certainly will, given the nature of the educational enterprise, diversity of perspectives represented on campus, perceptions about the stakes involved in higher education for all parties, and the broader social environment in which higher education take places. It is our hope that pursuing these recommendations will help professionals better prepare themselves and their campus communities to take advantage of these situations as opportunities for genuine learning and development, both personal and organizational, rather than to have the situations overwhelm the available opportunity.

The first recommendation may seem to stand in contrast to the general focus of this book, but it is important to point out that legal considerations are only one framework for thinking about these matters—and perhaps not the most important one. Colleges and universities are first and foremost institutions of learning, and that needs to be at the forefront of any planning, program, practice, or response. We might also consider other lenses in our thinking. Social justice and healing are two perspectives which come to mind in addition to the educational and legal frameworks. Our most constructive and powerful way forward is not likely through essentializing any one lens but rather through a thoughtful and purposeful integration of multiple ways of framing questions and responses.

A second recommendation is to be proactive and inclusive in articulating or revisiting statements of your institution's principles related to First Amendment freedoms. It can be tempting for any number of reasons to seek comfort in pre-packaged, politically popular so-called 'best practices' boilerplates such as what is commonly referred to as the Chicago Principles (Stone, Bertrand, Olinto, Siegler, Strauss, Warren, & Woodward, 2014). The most promising pathways to principles which will balance the values held by colleges and universities with regard to both inclusion and support for First Amendment freedoms are those which reflect the local institutional context, history, traditions, culture, and populations (Ben-Porath, 2018). It is vitally important that the effort to bring forward these principles assures plentiful opportunities for the meaningful participation of students, including students from historically minoritized populations, in order to increase the likelihood that principles articulated have wide campus support. We find ourselves in complete agreement with Ben-Porath's (2018) observation:

> Students may be young and have a lot to learn—that's why they come to college—but they demand that we fulfill the promise of democratic deliberation and equal dignity to all. They deserve our attention. Endorsing premade rules shuts them out.
>
> (para. 14)

A third recommendation is to invest time in professional development intended to strengthen both campus climate and institutional preparedness. Offering students, staff, and faculty opportunities to develop and strengthen skills in intercultural communication, conflict resolution, social change leadership, free speech and First Amendment freedoms, and other related knowledge and skills bases can lead to numerous benefits for the individuals involved and for the campus community. It is likely that there are people on your campus, if not at nearby campuses, who have a great deal to offer in the way of facilitating these developmental programs.

Fifth, and related to the fourth, is the recommendation to establish protocols and provide training to staff (including law enforcement officers) and faculty on how to respond when protests occur on campus. Many campuses either do not have these assets in place or have not maintained them as current. The protocols and training are more likely to be beneficial if they explicitly address both free speech and inclusion goals.

Sixth, foster a 'listen first' leadership culture. There can sometimes be an inclination, particularly on the part of senior administrative staff, to want to move as quickly as possible to explain why it is that things stand as they do or are playing out as they are. Remember, the system which is behind those answers is likely to be seen as complicit, if not causal, of the problem by some involved in the situation. It can be powerfully important to listen first before advancing answers—or excuses or placations as some may see them. Thoughtful listening and reiteration of what is understood from what has been heard may help in affirming honest intent and being sure that all parties involved have a shared understanding of the problem at hand, even if they have not yet identified common ground for moving forward.

A seventh recommendation is to review extant institutional practices and policies to identify any potential problematic areas. Closely scrutinize any requirements for prior approval in co-curricular programs to help assure that they are not subject to claims of prior restraint. Consider campus space reservation regulations to be sure they are content neutral in compliance with the constructs of reasonable time, place, and manner restrictions. If your campus has free speech zones, take a long hard look at whether or not that is a position your institution wishes to defend in court. Give similar thought to any college or university policies related to speech, particularly being on the lookout for any references to hate speech or equivalent terms which may be overly broad.

Our eighth and final recommendation relates to positions on campus which may have a particular responsibility for responding to incidences of biased or hateful behavior. This may include individual positions such as hate-bias response coordinators (Brown, 2017) or bias response teams (PEN America, 2019). It is not our purpose to speak against such positions. They may offer very important benefits to the campus communities they serve. However, it can be particularly important that anyone involved in these sorts of positions has thorough knowledge and awareness regarding the importance of promoting both inclusion and free speech. Any college or university that includes these positions must accept a responsibility to assure that training is available and to provide support for the people doing this difficult but important work on campus.

LOOKING AHEAD

Recall the discussion early in the chapter about the behavior of members of a national fraternity chapter at the University of Oklahoma and that institution's response to the behavior. You were asked before to reflect on that decision and determine whether or not it was the correct action and what led you to that opinion. Now, having read through this chapter, we ask that you repeat that reflection. Has either your view or reasoning changed? Hopefully the key concepts, important cases, and broad lessons shared in this chapter will be helpful to higher education professionals and others who are involved in the contemporary context of the co-curricular lives of students on college and university campuses. In addition, the information may be helpful to these same people in looking forward to what may be on the horizon of law and higher education. What might that include? The answers are myriad, but let us take a moment to explore just one of the possible answers—the emergence of cases involving the rights of students who identify as trans. There is currently very little in the way of legal guidance in this area, and what little is out there relates primarily to employment law. Office of Civil Rights policy has shifted with changes in administration so it remains unclear whether or not Title IX considerations are in play. Policies related to student records, housing, bathrooms and locker rooms, and participation in student organizations and activities are all areas in which there could be legal dispute based on First Amendment claims (Perdue, 2014). How might we use what has been presented in this chapter to develop policies, programs, and policies that advance the educational mission of our institution, embrace our value of inclusivity, and support First Amendment freedoms across our co-curricular offerings?

REFERENCES

Abbott v. Pastides, No. 17-1853 (4th Cir. 2018).

Adams, L. (2017, October 19). Heckling is a staple of controversial campus speeches: Should colleges intervene? *The Chronicle of Higher Education*. Retrieved from www.chronicle.com/article/Heckling-Is-a-Staple-of/241504

Andrews, T. M. (2017, April 19). Federal judge stops Auburn from canceling white nationalist Richard Spencer speech: Protests and a scuffle greet him. *Washington Post*. Retrieved from www.washingtonpost.com/news/morning-mix/wp/2017/04/19/federal-judge-stops-auburn-from-canceling-white-nationalists-speech-violence-erupts/?utm_term=.1f4bca586bd5

Aschoff, E. (2019, March 1). In Oxford, the protest is over . . . but "the conversation is not going away." *ESPN*. Retrieved from www.espn.com/mens-college-basketball/story/_/id/26105323/ole-miss-basketball-players-kneeling-protest-led-positive-conversations-oxford-mississippi

Associated Press (2019, February 15). UNC–Chapel Hill drops case of student who bloodied Silent Sam statue. *WFAO*. Retrieved from www.wfae.org/post/unc-chapel-hill-drops-case-student-who-bloodied-silent-sam-statue#stream/0

Bair v. Shippensburg University, 280 F. Supp. 2d 357 (M.D. Pa. 2003).

Bauman, D., & Turnage, C. (2017, August 22). We're tracking Confederate monuments: Tell us what's on your campus. *The Chronicle of Higher Education*. Retrieved from www.chronicle.com/article/We-re-Tracking-Confederate/240967

Bayless v. Martine, 430 F.2d 872 (5th Cir. 1970).

Beassie, R., & Gomez, F. (2015). In J. C. Sun, N. H. Hutchens, & B. A. Sponsler (Eds). *Responding to campus protests: A practitioner resource*. Cleveland, OH: Education Law Association & NASPA-Student Affairs Administrators in Higher Education.

Ben-Porath, S. (2018, December 11). Against endorsing the Chicago Principles. *InsideHigherEd*. Retrieved from www.insidehighered.com/views/2018/12/11/what-chicago-principles-miss-when-it-comes-free-speech-and-academic-freedom-opinion/

Board of Regents of University of Wisconsin System v. Southworth, 529 U.S. 217 (2000).

Brock, M. D., Michelmore, M., & Horowitz, S. (2018, September 6). Why universities should be on the front lines of the monument wars. *Washington Post*. Retrieved from www.washingtonpost.com/outlook/2018/09/06/why-universities-should-be-front-lines-monument-wars/?utm_term=.c98a95070c05

Brown, S. (2017, November 28). Why the U. of Maryland is hiring a "hate-bias response coordinator." *The Chronicle of Higher Education*. Retrieved from www.chronicle.com/article/Why-the-U-of-Maryland-Is/241904

Central Hudson Gas & Electric Cor. v. Public Service Commission of New York, 447 U.S. 557 (1980).

Chaplinsky v. New Hampshire, 315 U.S. 568 (1942).

Chemerinsky, E., & Gillman, H. (2017). *Free speech on campus*. New Haven, CT: Yale University Press.

Christian Legal Society v. Martinez, 561 U.S. 661 (2010).

Ciemnecki, D. (2018, September 16). Majority of Americans value free speech over protection from offensive language. *WGBH*. Retrieved from www.wgbh.org/news/education/2018/09/16/majority-of-americans-value-free-speech-over-protection-from-offensive-language

Clark v. Community for Creative Non-Violence, 468 U.S. 288 (1984).

Cohen v. California, 403 U.S. 15 (1971).

College Republicans at San Francisco State v. Reed, 523 F. Supp. 2d 1005 (N.D. Cal. 2007).

College Republicans of University of Washington v. Cauce, 2018 WL 804497 (W.D. Wash. February 9, 2018).

Deconto, J. J., & Blinder, A. (2018, April 21). Silent Sam statue is toppled at University of North Carolina. *New York Times*. Retrieved from www.nytimes. com/2018/08/21/us/unc-silent-sam-monument-toppled.html

Doe v. University of Michigan, 721 F. Supp. 852 (E.D. Mich. 1989).

Espinosa, L. L., Crandall, J. R., & Wilkinson, P. (2018, April 9). *Free speech and campus inclusion: A survey of college presidents*. Washington, DC: American Council on Education. Retrieved from www.higheredtoday. org/2018/04/09/free-speech-campus-inclusion-survey-college-presidents/

Fernandez, M., & Pérez-Peña, R. (2015 March 10). As two Oklahoma students are expelled for racist chant, Sigma Alpha Epsilon vows wider inquiry. *New York Times*. Retrieved from www.nytimes.com/2015/03/11/us/university-of-oklahoma-sigma-alpha-epsilon-racist-fraternity-video.html

Gallup (2018). *Free expression on campus: What college students think about first amendment issues*. Washington, DC: Gallup.

Good v. Associated Students of the Univ. of Washington, 542 P. 2d 762 (Wash. 1975).

Grayned v. City of Rockford, 408 U.S. 104 (1972).

Harassment law and legal definition (2016). *USLegal.com*. Retrieved from https:// definitions.uslegal.com/h/harassment/

Healy v. James, 408 U.S. 169 (1972).

Hutchens, N. H. (2017, June 27). New legislation may make free speech on campus less free. *The Conversation*. Retrieved from https://theconversation.com/ new-legislation-may-make-free-speech-on-campus-less-free-77609

Hutchens, N. H. (2019, April 9). Campus free speech laws being enacted in many states, but some may do more harm than good. *The Conversation*. Retrieved from https://theconversation.com/campus-free-speech-laws-being-enacted-in-many-states-but-some-may-do-more-harm-than-good-114551?utm_source=twitter&utm_medium=twitterbutton

Iota XI Chapter of Sigma Chi Fraternity v. George Mason University (1991). 773 F. Supp. 792, 795 (E.D. Va. 1991), aff'd 993 F. 2d 386 (4th Cir. 1993).

Jacobellis v. Ohio, 378 U.S. 184 (1964).

Jacobs, J. (2019, January 15). U.N.C chancellor to leave early after ordering removal of Silent Sam statue's base. *New York Times*. Retrieved from www. nytimes.com/2019/01/15/us/silent-sam-statue-removal-unc.html

Kampis, J. (2018 May 21). Critics say Texas universities don't protect free speech. *Texas Monitor*. Retrieved from https://texasmonitor.org/critics-say-texas-universities-dont-protect-free-speech/

Kaplin, W. A., & Lee, B. A. (2006). *The law of higher education* (4th ed.). San Francisco: Jossey-Bass.

Kaplin, W. A., & Lee, B. A. (2013). *The law of higher education* (5th ed.). San Francisco: Jossey-Bass.

Korn, M. (2019, February 14). Colleges continue to confront blackface on campus. *Wall Street Journal*. Retrieved from www.wsj.com/articles/colleges-continue-to-confront-blackface-on-campus-11550167774

Kurtz, S., Manley, J., & Butcher, J. (2017, January 30). *Campus free speech: A legislative proposal*. Phoenix, AZ: Goldwater Institute. Retrieved from https://goldwaterinstitute.org/wp-content/uploads/cms_page_media/2017/2/2/X_Campus%20Free%20Speech%20Paper.pdf

Lake, P. (2009). *Beyond discipline: Managing the modern higher education environment*. Bradenton, FL: Hierophant Enterprises.

Lake, P. (2011). *Foundations of higher education law and policy: Basic legal rules, concepts, and principles for student affairs*. Washington, DC: NASPA.

Lanmon, L. (2017, November 29). Editorial in Texas State student newspaper condemned as "racist." *KXAN*. Retrieved from www.kxan.com/news/local/hays/students-claim-editorial-posted-in-texas-state-student-newspaper-is-racist/1031408166

Larimer, S. (2017, June 20). Senate hearing examines free speech on college campuses after incidents at UC-Berkeley, Middlebury. *Washington Post*. Retrieved from www.washingtonpost.com/news/grade-point/wp/2017/06/20/senate-hearingexamines-free-speech-on-college-campuses-after-incidents-at-uc-berkeley-middlebury

Legal Information Institute (n.d.). *Establishment Clause*. Ithaca, NY: Cornell Law School. Retrieved from www.law.cornell.edu/wex/establishment_clause

Lemon v. Kurtzman, 403 U.S. 602 (1971).

Lewis v. Wilson, 253 F.3d (8th Cir. 2001).

Mangan, K. (2018a, January 31). Texas lawmakers weigh the limits of free speech on campus. *The Chronicle of Higher Education*. Retrieved from www.chronicle.com/article/Texas-Lawmakers-Weigh-the/242405

Mangan, K. (2018b, April 12). Seething racial tensions prompt sit in at Texas State University U. student center. *The Chronicle of Higher Education*. Retrieved from www.chronicle.com/article/Seething-Racial-Tensions/243109

Mangan, K. (2019a, April 2). 2 students face criminal charges after calling border agents "murderers." *The Chronicle of Higher Education*. Retrieved from www.chronicle.com/article/2-Students-Face-Criminal/246038

Mangan, K. (2019b, March 2). Trumps says he'll sign order requiring colleges to protect free speech. *The Chronicle of Higher Education*. Retrieved from www.chronicle.com/article/Trump-Says-He-ll-Sign-Order/245812www.chronicle.com/article/Trump-Says-He-ll-Sign-Order/245812

Miller v. California, 413 U.S. 15 (1973).

New, J. (2015a, March 9). Fraternity caught on video singing racist song. *Inside Higher Ed*. Retrieved from www.insidehighered.com/quicktakes/2015/03/09/fraternity-caught-video-singing-racist-song

New, J. (2015b, March 30). SAE at sea. *Inside Higher Ed*. Retrieved from www. insidehighered.com/news/2015/03/30/u-oklahoma-chapter-learned-racist-song-sae-leadership-cruise

Ohlheiser, A. (2015, April 6). Clemson's Sigma Alpha Epsilon fraternity place on probation for "Cripmas" party. *Washington Post*. Retrieved from www.washingtonpost.com/news/grade-point/wp/2015/04/06/clemsons-sigma-alpha-epsilon-fraternity-placed-on-probation-for-cripmas-party/?noredirect=on&utm_term=.888fda1ecf2f

OSU Student Alliance v. Ray, 699 F.3d 1053 (9th Cir. 2012).

Papish v. Board of Curators of the University of Missouri, 410 U.S. 667, 670 (1973).

Patel, V. (2018, May 1). Why a protestor at Chapel Hill doused a Confederate monument in red ink and blood. *The Chronicle of Higher Education*. Retrieved from www.chronicle.com/article/Why-a-Protester-at-Chapel-Hill/243296

PEN America (2017, June 15). *And campus for all: Diversity, inclusion, and freedom of speech at U.S. universities*. New York: Author. Retrieved from https://pen.org/wp-content/uploads/2017/06/PEN_campus_report_06.15.2017.pdf

PEN America (2019, April 2). *Chasm in the classroom: Campus free speech in a divided America*. New York: Author. Retrieved from https://pen.org/wp-content/uploads/2019/04/2019-PEN-Chasm-in-the-Classroom-v3.pdf

Perdue, T. J. (2014). Top 5 trans* issues for colleges and universities. Records, housing, bathrooms, locker rooms, and athletics. Paper presented at 2014 NACUA Annual Conference. Berwyn, PA: Association of Title IX Administrators. Retrieved from https://cdn.atixa.org/website-media/o_atixa/wp-content/uploads/2012/01/18121710/TOP-5-TRANS-ISSUES-FOR-COLLEGES-AND-UNIVERSITIES-RECORDS-HOUSING-BATHROOMS-LOCKER-ROOMS-AND-ATHLETICS.pdf

Planned Parenthood of Columbia/Willamette, Inc., et al. v. American Coalition of Life Advocates, et al., 290 F.3d 1058 (9th Cir. 2002).

R.A.V. v. City of St. Paul, 505 U.S. 377 (1992).

Rock for Life-UMBC v. Hrabowski, 411 Fed. A'ppx. 541 (4th Cir. 2010).

Rueb, E. S. (2019, March 8). Ole Miss student and faculty groups vote to relocate Confederate statue. *New York Times*. Retrieved from www.nytimes.com/2019/03/08/us/ole-miss-confederate-statue.html

Shamloo v. Mississippi State Board of Trustees, 620 F.2d 516 (5th Cir. 1980).

Spencer, H., & Stolberg, S. G. (2017, Aug. 11). White nationalists march on University of Virginia. *New York Times*, https://www.nytimes.com/2017/08/11/us/white-nationalists-rally-charlottesville-virginia.html

Stone, G. R., Bertrand, M., Olinto, A., Siegler, M., Strauss, D. A., Warren, K. W., & Woodward, A. (2014). *Report on the committee on freedom of expression*. Chicago: University of Chicago. Retrieved from https://provost.uchicago.edu/sites/default/files/documents/reports/FOECommitteeReport.pdf

Sun, J. C., Hutchens, N. H., & Breslin, J. D. (2013). A virtual land of confusion with college students' online speech: Introducing the curricular nexus test. *University of Pennsylvania Journal of Constitutional Law, 16*(1), pp. 49–96.

Thomason, A. (2017, September 25). Sessions adds to Trumpian chorus on campus speech limits. *The Chronicle of Higher Education*. Retrieved from www.chronicle.com/article/Jeff-Sessions-Adds-to-Trumpian/241288

Tinker v. Des Moines Independent Community School District (1969).

Toler, L. (2015, March 10). A racist stunt got SAE suspended from Washington University in St. Louis, too. *Riverfront Times*. Retrieved from www.riverfronttimes.com/newsblog/2015/03/10/a-racist-stunt-got-sae-suspended-from-washington-university-in-st-louis-too

United States v. Alkhabaz aka Jake Baker, 104 F.3d 1492 (6th Cir. 1997).

United States v. Kelner, 534 F.2d 1020 (2d Cir. 1976).

UWM Post, Inc. v. Board of Regents of the University of Wisconsin System, 774 F. Supp. 1163 (E.D. Wis. 1991).

Virginia v. Black, 538 U.S. 343 (2003).

Ward v. Rock Against Racism, 491 U.S. 781 (1989).

Watts v. United States, 394 U.S. 705 (1969).

Widmar v. Vincent, 454 U.S. 263 (1981).

Yglesias, M. (2018, March 12). Everything we think about the political correctness debate is wrong. *Vox*. Retrieved from www.vox.com/policy-and-politics/2018/3/12/17100496/political-correctness-data

Chapter Four

Digital Communication
Advancing Technologies, New Challenges, and Free Speech on Campus

Hector is angry, confused, embarrassed, and to be honest more than a little frightened. Pictures of him in a locker room shower on campus are being circulated through social media, and he is also receiving anonymous email messages which are threatening to share additional pictures even more widely and with his family if Hector does not step down from his position as president of the Hispanic Republicans student group on his campus. The messages include insults about his body and his political beliefs. As if things were not already weird enough, it seems like the email messages only show up right as he is about to head into a campus building like his classrooms, labs, or residence hall. It is almost like whoever is sending them knows where he is at and is trying to make it really hard on him to function on campus. Now more people are getting involved in the online discussion. Some are calling out whoever is posting the pics, and others are saying it serves Hector right for being a tool for those who treat his people so badly. Really? He just wants this to stop, and he feels like he needs help. Hector speaks with his resident assistant, and they speak with their resident director and with the assistant dean for residential life on campus. They are empathetic but indicate there is not much they can do as the messages are coming in anonymously. Hector is beginning to think that the only option he has is to step down from his leadership position and to give up working out at campus recreation for a while.

The way in which the intersection of higher education institutions' interests in supporting both free speech and inclusive campus communities plays out in digital communication environments is an exemplar of the truism: there are few things more certain than the uncertainty of what lies ahead. The tensions which are sometimes perceived between these two interests reflect underlying societal considerations of computer-mediated communication. As Ben-Porath (2018) points out,

> The growing influence of digital communication, including social media, has given rise to competing interpretations about its role in democratic life. Some, like Habermas, have described the "disintegration of the public sphere," a sadly fragmented set of debates separated by filter bubbles and tribal domains. Others see digital communication as democratizing, and specifically as making space for a thoughtful attentive media where public intellectuals can profess their views to a reading audience, and where people of diverse backgrounds and worldviews can develop a following.
>
> (p. 2)

Coupled with these societal variations in interpretations is the dizzying pace of change in technology. Moore's Law, which posits that the number of transistors which can be mounted on a chip doubles about every two years, is evidenced in the rapidity with which technological innovations take place. Personal computers made their way on the world stage just 40 years ago, and it took only 30 years for smartphones to appear in the marketplace (Berman & Dorrier, 2016).

In addition to the differing perspectives on digital communication and rapid pace of change, an additional consideration related to cyberspeech and free speech in higher education is the ubiquity of digital communication. Nearly 90% of people in the United States between the ages of 18 and 29 use some form of social media (Pew Research Center, 2018) with variations in social medial platform use across age groups (Marvin, 2019). There is some evidence that social media use is peaking (Marvin, 2019), but it is peaking at significant levels. College students are particularly avaricious consumers of digital communication (Jones, Johnson-Yale, Millermaier, & Seoane Pérez, 2009), though their choices of platforms shift notably and quickly (Marvin, 2018).

Griffin (2017), drawing on an observation made by journalist Thomas Friedman, identifies 2007 as a pivotal year in the modern pace of technological change with a number of advancements and adaptations that put much more technology into the hands of people for every day uses. Griffin opines that change is now coming so rapidly that we do not have time to adapt.

Not surprisingly, these new and rapidly expanding vehicles for speech are finding their way into law, policy, and attendant legal contests.

> The Internet and the World Wide Web opened virtually unlimited channels for communication and information for faculty, staff, and students for both pedagogical and personal purposes, and the

continued growth of computer and telecommunications-assisted distance learning, spawned new challenges regarding intellectual property, free speech, harassment, invasion of privacy, defamation, plagiarism, and a multitude of other issues.

(Kaplin, Lee, Hutchens, & Rooksby, 2019, p. 18)

There is no doubt the courts recognize the centrality of digital communication in matters of contemporary expression. As the Supreme Court opinion in *Packingham v. North Carolina* (2017, p. 137) states,

> While in the past there may have been difficulty in identifying the most important places (in a spatial sense) for the exchange of views, today the answer is clear. It is cyberspace—the "vast democratic forums of the Internet" in general, and social media in particular. . . . [However,] in some respects, the law lags behind advances in technology.
>
> (Kaplin, Lee, Hutchens, & Rooksby, 2019, p. 419)

So, we have two important interests in higher education, which are sometimes seen as being at odds with one another, playing out in a politically charged environment of incredibly rapid change. There are also substantive differences in the experiences, expectations, and skill sets of various campus constituents across age ranges when it comes to digital communication. Top this off with a perception by many that there is not enough time for reflection and thoughtful deliberative action. What could go wrong? The answer, of course, is plenty.

Keeping in mind the rapidity with which circumstances are changing, this chapter will present information on the limited legal guidance available in the area of digital communication and free speech issues on college campuses and offer some general guidelines for helping campus communities navigate these issues. We will be presenting a working definition of digital communication, a term which will be used throughout the chapter to include an array of mediums of expression. Several areas of legal concern which have a bearing on free speech and digital communication on campuses are then addressed. The chapter next moves to a review of current legal cases related to free speech and social media in higher education before concluding with some early guidelines for consideration by those responsible for helping shape institutional policy, practice, and response.

DEFINING DIGITAL COMMUNICATION

Various terms are commonly used to discuss digital communication. Among these are email, social media, social network sites, and websites (Carr & Hayes, 2015). We have chosen to use the term *digital communication* for the purposes of this chapter. In doing so, we mean to include a broad range of expressive speech carried out through online technologies. This includes email, social media, texting, websites, and other extant platforms as well as modalities which have yet to emerge.

RELATED LEGAL CONCERNS

While the focus in this chapter and this book is on free speech, the topic is difficult to address with regard to social media and other forms of cyberspeech without also touching on two areas of related legal concerns. These are privacy and intellectual property.

It is not uncommon in disputes centered on digital communication for there to be a claim that the speech ought to be afforded protection as a matter of privacy. Ben-Porath (2018) points out the challenge of determining whether digital communication is public, private, or a hybrid.

> Along with unique forms of informality, access, control, and networking, online communications permit individuals to undertake various types of actions simultaneously. Thus, actions that could be considered social (sharing personal pictures), commercial (recommending a product), or civic (posting or sharing a post concerning social injustice), are increasing being conducted at the same time, on the same platforms, and with overlapping networks of individuals. . . . This phenomenon of context collapse has important implications: online interactions are not as strongly regulated through social norms on the one hand, and are harder to navigate according to context on the other. Therefore, along with greater access, digital communication provides ample possibilities for miscommunication and offense.
>
> (p. 15)

Much of the law around privacy considerations is found in state statutes and, therefore, it is commonly applicable to both private and public higher education institutions. In addition, the Fourth Amendment of the Constitution provides for the right of privacy against unreasonable searches and seizures from person, home, papers, or effects. This protection applies at all public institutions and, like free speech and other First Amendment freedoms, may be extended to members of private college and university communities through codes, contracts, policies, or practices.

In addition to regulation by state and federal governments, another important development in the area of privacy is occurring as a result of international action. The European Union's General Data Protection Regulation (GDPR) is intended to protect the data-privacy of citizens of European

Union (EU) nations as well as to describe the data-privacy responsibilities of organizations doing business in EU nations. The GDRP specifically identifies three roles: the person to whom the data are related; the entity which controls how the data are used; and the entity which processes the data. Higher education institutions offering programs or services in European Union (EU) nations, marketing their U.S.-based services or programs to citizens of EU nations, or with citizens of EU nations as members as students, staff, or faculty could be held accountable for compliance (Raths, 2018).

One construct emerging from the passage and implementation of the GDPR and Google Spain SL, *Google Inc v Agencia Española de Protección de Datos*, Mario Costeja González (2014), a subsequent court case in Spain, is the 'right to be forgotten' (Right to be forgotten, n.d.) or the right of erasure. What does this mean?

> Personal data must be erased immediately where the data are no longer needed for their original processing purpose, or the data subject has withdrawn his consent and there is no other legal ground for processing, the data subject has objected and there are no overriding legitimate grounds for the processing, or erasure is required to fulfil a statutory obligation under the EU law or the right of the Member States. In addition, data must naturally be erased if the processing itself was against the law in the first place.
>
> The controller is therefore on the one hand automatically subject to statutory erasure obligations, and must, on the other hand, comply with the data subject's right to erasure. The law does not describe how the data must be erased in individual cases. The decisive element is that as a result it is no longer possible to discern personal data without disproportionate effort. It is sufficient if the data media has been physically destroyed, or if the data is permanently over-written using special software.
>
> In addition, the right to be forgotten is found in Art. 17(2) of the GDPR. If the controller has made the personal data public, and if one of the above reasons for erasure exists, he must take reasonable measures, considering the circumstances, to inform all other controllers in data processing that all links to this personal data, as well as copies or replicates of the personal data, must be erased.
>
> (Right to be forgotten, n.d., pp. 2–4)

The full impact of the GDPR and the right to be forgotten are yet to be determined for higher education. It also remains to be seen whether the underlying ideas of data ownership and rights to control of data which inform the DGPR make their way into legislation in the United States.

95

Intellectual property laws, in particular laws defining and protecting intellectual property rights, also may have an impact on the way colleges and universities craft digital communication policies that could in turn have an impact on speech. The Digital Millennium Copyright Act of 1998, the TEACH Act of 2002, and the Higher Education Opportunity Act of 2008 are all examples of such legislation which specifically addresses the responsibilities of post-secondary institutions with regard to protecting intellectual property rights in cyberspace.

CURRENT FREE SPEECH AND DIGITAL COMMUNICATION HIGHER EDUCATION CASES

Having offered a working definition of digital communication and high-lighted privacy and intellectual property as two related areas of legal concern, we now turn our attention to a central concern of this chapter. What information is available to use about the ways in which courts view how free speech issues are to be considered when it comes to digital communication in higher education settings? Our discussion, which keeps in mind the distinctions between applicable law in private and public higher education settings, will be structured around two key campus constituencies who receive significantly different treatment under the law with regard to free speech—employees and students.

Employees

The Supreme Court ruled in *Garcetti v. Ceballos* (2006) that public employees' private speech on matters of public compelling interest are protected, but speech in which they engage as part of their public duties does not carry similar protections. Free speech may, or may not, be provided to employees at private higher education institutions as a function of contract or (in some instances) state law.

The *Garcetti* finding raises concern for public higher education employees generally, but it is of particular concern for faculty members at public institutions for whom speech in their areas of expertise has long been seen as protected both as a matter of the First Amendment and as a matter of academic freedom. Similar protections are commonly afforded to faculty members at private institutions as a function of contract, institutional policy, or state statute.

The constructs of academic freedom and freedom of speech are closely aligned in the minds of many, but there are important distinctions between the two. Academic freedom rests in no small part on contract law and sometimes state statute buttressed by academic custom and some support from the courts. In particular, in *Sweezy v. New Hampshire* (1957), *Shelton v. Tucker* (1960), *Griswold v. Connecticut* (1965), and *Keyishian v. Board of Regents* (1967), the Supreme Court laid out a series of decisions which advanced the argument that academic freedom is an important aspect of free speech in higher education settings. However, Supreme Court decisions in *Pickering v. Board of Education* (1968) and *Gracetti v. Ceballos* (2006), which shifted ground to broader public employee speech language, give reason for a degree of uncertainty about the current standing of academic freedom as a form of free speech in the eyes of the courts (Kaplin, Lee, Hutchens, & Rooksby, 2019).

How specifically have considerations of free speech in digital communication played out in courts? We do not have a great number of settled cases to explore. Dr. Steven G. Salaita was offered a faculty position at the University of Illinois, and he accepted the offer. It was subsequently rescinded when several of his comments on Twitter about Israel came to light (Gardner, 2015). Salaita filed two suits against the institution on both contractual and free speech grounds, but the parties agreed to an out of court settlement for nearly $900K before the cases came to trial. In a rare case in this area that actually went to trial, *McAdams v. Marquette University* (2018), Professor McAdams was disciplined by Marquette University for comments made on his personal blog about the way in which a graduate student teaching courses in another department handled their interaction with a student in class. The post, which alleged that a conservative viewpoint was being stifled in campus conversation, went viral. The graduate student was targeted with offensive messages. The initial case brought by Professor Adams was summarily dismissed on the grounds that he had agreed to the university's disciplinary procedures as a term of his employment. However, in taking up the case, the Wisconsin Supreme Court took issue with the procedural finding (arguing that the university had not provided the employee with due process) but also found that the professor's speech was protected in that it was private speech (meaning made in public but not in the area of faculty expertise, though on a university-related subject) and did not offer any evidence that the employee was unfit for his position.

The McAdams case points to one of the challenges related to free speech and employees in post-secondary education. Where is 'work' when people are doing things in the office, across campus, on their smartphones as they travel, or from home (Kaplin, Lee, Hutchens, & Rooksby, 2019)? The question is not limited just to employees and work. A similar challenge exists, as we will discuss in the next section, with regard to where the boundaries of campus lie when it comes to student behavior.

The question about where is work has direct implications for expectations of privacy. As an example, in *United States v. Soderstrand* (2005) and a related case brought by Professor Soderstrand against the Board of Regents of Oklahoma Agricultural and Mechanical Colleges, Dr. Soderstrand argued that his privacy rights were violated by university employees. Child pornography was found on CDS in a locked box in university storage space. University security employees later entered his office and seized the hard drive from his office computer and his personal laptop which was connected to the university network. They did so without warrant and without his permission. The court found that Dr. Soderstrand had no reasonable expectation of privacy given that he was using university assets including the storage space, his work computer, and the university computing network.

Students

Having addressed important cases involving free speech and digital communication for those employed at colleges and universities, we now turn our attention to cases involving free speech and other First Amendment freedoms for those who are enrolled. Many of today's college students (though not all) make the rest of us look like Ludites when it comes to digital communication. As Nott (2017) observes, "Most college students today have grown up surrounded by social media. An enormous amount of their 'speech' takes place on digital platforms such as Facebook, Twitter, and Instagram" (p. 1). Just how ubiquitous is the use of digital communication by students? Jones, Johnson-Yale, Millermaier, and Seoane Pérez (2009) report nearly 100% of students use email and social media.

It is not just how much students use digital communication that makes it a particularly important arena to consider relative to free speech issues. Gallup and the Knight Foundation (Gallup, 2018), in a 2017 study of the digital media experiences of college students related to free speech, found students more likely to use social media to discuss political and social issues (57%) rather than public areas of campus (43%). It is not clear if this is just a reflection of students' affinity for social media or due to their perceptions about campus environment. Students responding to the 2017 study were less likely than students responding to a similar study in 2016 to see social media conversations as civil (only 37% see it as usually so) and more likely to say it is too easy for folks to say things anonymously (83%). In the 2017 study, a majority (60%) of students said social media stifles free expression because folks block views with which they disagree, and a similar majority (59%) noted it stifles free expression because folks are afraid of being attacked or shamed by those who disagree. Interestingly, students who identify as Republicans were more likely to see social media as civil and less likely to see the negatives. Over 80% of students said the Internet is responsible for an increase in hate speech (see Mangan (2018b) for examples of such incidents), and nearly 70% stated social media platforms like Facebook and Twitter should be responsible for limiting hate speech on their platforms. Students identifying as Republicans were far less likely to agree with the latter.

Nott rightfully points out,

> Naturally, the prevalence of social media on college campuses presents the following question: at a public university or college, do officials and administrators have the right to discipline, punish, or expel students based on the content of their social media posts?
>
> (2017, p. 1)

This section of the chapter will present what evidence there is from recent court cases relative to that question and other related legal concerns.

Speech

There are a small number of cases already which address questions of students' free speech and digital communication. Two of these cases address matters of student speech related to their experiences in academic programs. Amanda Tatro was an undergraduate student enrolled in a mortuary sciences program at the University of Minnesota when she posted several comments on her Facebook page stating she "want[ed] to stab a certain someone in the throat with a trocar" (Tatro v. University of Minnesota, 2011, p. 512) and in which she made unflattering remarks about the cadavers with which students were working in the lab. The university disciplined her for both disruption and failure to adhere to the professional standards articulated by the program. The court sided with the university in *Tatro v. University of Minnesota* (2011). However, on appeal, the court did not agree with the university that it was on solid ground when arguing that the disruption charge was warranted or that the comment about the trocar constituted a true threat, but it affirmed that the discipline was warranted in light of the violation of the program's professional standards (Tatro v. University of Minnesota, 2012). *Keefe v. Adams* (2016), which was discussed in Chapter 2, presents another instance in which the court found that disciplining a student for violating professional conduct through speech about classmates or patients is warranted. It is worth noting that in both of these instances the programs had established professional conduct standards which were made known to students as part of their enrollment in the program.

At least one case has also addressed student speech, digital communication, and the fighting words doctrine. Darren Drahota, a student at the University of Nebraska–Lincoln, exchanged a lengthy series of email messages with Professor William Avery about a variety of topics (State v. Drahota, 2010). Drahota's emails, which were sent anonymously, contained elements that were friendly, but they also included content that was angry, profane, and discriminatory. Professor Avery asked Drahota to end the email exchange, but a short time later, Professor Avery received several anonymous messages that were "laced with provocative and insulting rhetoric and—with the Iraq war as a background—suggested that [the professor] was a traitor and that he sympathized with Al Qaeda" (State v. Drahota, 2010, p. 629). It was these latter assertions which led Professor Avery to contact local law enforcement who, after discovering he was responsible for the anonymous messages, charged Drahota with breach of the peace. The court maintained the established position that speech cannot be curtailed just because it "inflicts emotional injury, annoys, offends, or angers another person" (p. 636). It decided that the speech was protected and did not fall under the fighting words doctrine as Drahota was at some distance from Avery when sending the messages and the final messages were sent anonymously so there was no likelihood that the emails could trigger an immediate violent reaction.

The question of harassment is featured in two other cases related to student speech and digital communication. Recall that harassment law developed under application of Title VII of the Civil Rights Act of 1964 (governing employment) and Title IX of the Educational Amendments (governing schools that receive federal funds) prohibits behavior which, either through quid pro quo arrangements or by creating a hostile, intimidating, or offensive environment, blocks equal opportunities in workplace or educational settings, respectively. While Title IX addresses equity based on gender, the idea of harassment has been extended to other protected groups (for example. harassment based on race) based on Title VI of Civil Rights Act of 1964. In *Koeppel v Romano* (2017), the court found that Valencia College's suspension of a male student for harassing a female student via email (having sent her more than 100 messages in a single evening) was not a violation of that student's free speech because the university had a legitimate educational interest in assuring the rights of all students to pursue educational opportunity. It also held that this legitimate interest extended to speech which arguably took place off campus. However, in *Yeasin v. University of Kansas* (2015), the court ruled that a student could not be expelled for tweeting harassing comments about his former girlfriend because the campus code referenced only such behavior taking place on campus and the institution could not prove that this was the case.

Another court case, *Feminist Majority Foundation v. Hurley*, is one that bears close monitoring. Members of Feminists United, a registered student organization at the University of Mary Washington, were being harassed online by anonymous comments on Yik Yak—a now defunct digital communication platform (Jaschik, 2018). The students reported the situation to officials at the university and asked that they offer assistance, including blocking Yik Yak from being able to be accessed from university servers. The university spoke out against the harassment and conducted listening forums to hear from the students about what they were experiencing, but it resisted their calls for Yik Yak to be blocked. The students filed suit against the university, and a federal appeals court is allowing the case to proceed after it was initially thrown out by a lower court's ruling. The university's argument centered on its concerns about protecting free speech, but the appeals court pointed out that true threats are not a protected form of speech and that the university may have had reasonable alternatives it could have pursued to prevent harm to its students (a compelling interest). What's also important to draw from this case is that the federal appellate court considered the public university as having control over the harasser. Although the university asserted the Yaks were anonymous, the court was unimpressed with the university's efforts because it "never sought to discern whether it could identify the harassers . . . even though some of those messages were facilitated by (i.e., posted through the use of) [the university's] network" (p. 688). This court's analysis presents us with two new administrative practice steps. Anonymous online postings do not release the university from liability and allow campuses to distance themselves from the harassing action. As this court states, the university still had substantial control through its disciplinary process potentially over some of the harassers. Also, the case reminds us that our campuses carry a lot of data, and while sleuth-like technology practices may be required, these investigatory processes, which some might argue resemble a criminal investigation, are expected of campuses.

The experience of Harley Barber while a student at the University of Alabama is also worth considering. Ms. Barber, who was at the time a member of the campus' chapter of Alpha Phi sorority, posted several videos on social media in which she made use of derogatory and inflammatory racial language and appeared to speak disparagingly of civil rights icon Dr. Martin Luther King, Jr. (Gajanan, 2018; Robinson, 2018). When word of those videos spread on campus, Ms. Barber began receiving a barrage of messages in various forms that strongly expressed disapproval of her behavior and, in at least some instances, made use of similarly vile epithets and threats. Her sorority expelled her as a member, and Ms. Barber left the University of Alabama saying she had been expelled. Ms. Barber's mother subsequently shared public comments decrying her daughter's behavior and indicating both her daughter and their family accepted the expulsion (Robinson, 2018). The action of the sorority in expelling Ms. Barber may have eased her willingness to accept the expulsion from the institution, but what if she had not? What if she had chosen to fight it on the grounds of free speech and what if, while remaining enrolled, she had pressed a claim against the University of Alabama for failing to protect her from harassment along the lines of the women in the Feminist United case? These hypothetical questions point to some of the complexities of balancing free speech and inclusion on college campuses in an epoch of digital communication.

Shifting to obscenity, a form of speech not protected by First Amendment rights, there is ample reason for higher education institutions to play close attention to the way in which their computers and their networks are used. Communications Decency Act of 1996 Title V of the Telecommunications Act of 1996 (47 U.S.C. §223 (2019)) makes it a crime to knowingly use the Internet to transmit obscenity or child pornography; other sections make anyone, who knowingly permits computer facilities under their control to be used in this way, liable for such acts. Given the age of many students on higher education campuses and the ages of their friends and folks with whom they may seek to associate, this is an area of law related to speech (in this instance, speech which is not protected) that ought to be of concern as a matter of law, education, and support for student success. There is cause for concern when one considers the extent to which college students are engaged in sexting behavior. Sexting may be "defined as the sending and/or receiving of sexually explicit content via electronic methods" (Florimbio, Brem, Garner, Grigorian, & Stuart, 2018, p. 205). A study by the National Campaign to Prevent Teen and Unplanned Pregnancy in 2008 reports that 87% of young adults had engaged at least once in sexting (as cited in Ingram, Macauda, Lauckner, & Robillard, 2019). Findings vary on the prevalence of this behavior amongst college students depending on the way in which the term is constructed and explored in any given study. Reyns, Henson, and Fisher (2014) report 17% of college students having sent nude or nearly nude pics of themselves via digital means and 23% having received such communication. In a similarly constructed study, Florimbio, Brem, Garner, Grigorian, and Stuart (2018) find nearly half of students (48.7%) had sent a naked picture and a slightly smaller proportion (40%) had received one. Interestingly, over half of the women students (51.8%) had sent a picture, but only 36% had requested one. Another study with a large national sample of college students notes 17% of students sent a nude picture of themselves using digital communication, and 23% have received such a picture (Reyns, Henson, & Fisher, 2014). Whether one takes the low number or the high number, we are talking about a lot of students engaging in risky behavior from a legal and developmental standpoint. One would have to be pretty naïve to believe that all of that behavior was taking place outside of the confines of the students' university computer networks. Given that students may not see their conduct as obscenity, pornography, or child pornography, it might be helpful for universities to frame their education and policy efforts in the language of students. Talk about sexting and the sharing, and talk about it in terms of healthy relationships, ethical and legal behavior, consent, and harassment. Colleges and universities are well-advised to keep in mind that it is not just students who engaged in these behaviors. While perhaps not as prevalent, higher education institutions have legal responsibility and liability whether this sort of behavior using their computing resources is undertaken by students, staff, or faculty.

Press

As noted in Chapter 3, freedom of speech and freedom of the press are closely related. Changes in technology triggering changes in laws related to what we understand as freedom of the press are nothing new. The advent of printing presses in the 15th century was perceived by church officials, who had tremendous sway on governments at the time, as a threat to their power, and they arranged to have licensing laws passed which restricted who could own and operate such devices (Chemerinsky & Gillman, 2017). The Privacy Protection Act of 1980 "limits the search and seizure of work product and other documentary materials of someone who is a news disseminator or publisher" (p. 1101), and courts have ruled that this protection extends to online material as well.

Privacy

It has been mentioned several times to this point that one of the arguments which is common in cases related to alleged infringement of speech is that state action impinges on a right of privacy. Such was the case in *United States v. Heckenkamp* (2007). It concerns a University of Wisconsin–Madison (UW) grad student who was suspected of hacking into a company's computer. The hack was through the UW network using the student's private computer which was searched remotely by university personnel when the matter was being investigated by law enforcement officials. Heckenkamp, the student, argued that the search constituted an invasion of his privacy. The court found that, indeed, such a search would be a violation of privacy rights were it not for the fact that the private computer was connected to the university network.

Student-athletes are another group where speech and privacy issues may arise related to digital communication. Specifically, the inclination of some institutions to monitor the social media presence of their student-athletes (Browning, 2012). Many institutions monitor the activities of their student-athletes on social media, and some even hire third-party vendors to do the monitoring on behalf of the institution (Thamel, 2012). A number of institutions require their student-athletes to surrender passwords for their social media accounts to their athletic department, but a growing number of states have laws or are considering laws banning institutions from making such a requirement (Snyder, Hutchens, Jones, & Sun, 2015; Thamel, 2012). Any intercollegiate athletic program which is monitoring the digital communication of its student-athletes would be wise to reconsider for at least two reasons. First, what would they do with any information they gather? It seems likely that any corrective or disciplinary action taken against a student on the basis of their online speech would open the program and the university to legal action related to restriction of free speech. A program defending itself in such an action might argue that they have a policy regarding the conduct expectation of student-athletes (not unlike the professional conduct codes discussed earlier in this chapter), but that line of reasoning could present a Pandora's Box of counterarguments that are potentially very problematic. Also, engaging in such monitoring brings with it an obligation to do so in consistent fashion. Failing that might lead to challenges from an athletics governance group (see the findings from the National Collegiate Athletics Association investigation of the University of North Carolina's program as an example) or in a court were there to be in instance in which a student-athlete came to harm or another person came to harm by a student-athlete where it could be argued that the program and institution could have or should have foreseen the potential for harm based on social media speech that it has a policy of monitoring.

CONCLUSION

What lessons can we draw from the limited legal decisions to date in the area of free speech and digital communication on college campuses, particularly given the interest in balancing the value of inclusion with support for free speech and other First Amendment freedoms? First, and perhaps most importantly, it helps to recognize

> although courts are committed to taking account of the unique aspects of each new communications technology, and allowing First Amendment law to grow and adapt in the process, thus far none of the basic principles . . . have been discarded or substantially transformed when applied to cyberspeech.
>
> (Kaplin, Lee, Hutchens, & Rooksby, 2019, p. 1097)

This constancy, at least to date, should provide a bit of comfort and needed time for those concerned with their institution's policies and practices in this area.

Another lesson which should help ease some tension is that there is legal authority and case law affirming an institution's right to establish use policies, hold members of the community accountable for those policies, and (with a policy in place and evidence of reasonable and consistent efforts of education and enforcement related to the policy) to not be held liable for unauthorized uses of its computers or networks. The Computer Fraud and Abuse Act, part of the Comprehensive Crime Control Act of 1984, makes it a crime for someone to access a computer or network without authorization or beyond the extent of their authorization to do so. Institutions should review their acceptable use policy regularly, include notice in the policy that they may be disciplined if their use is in violation, be sure that all members of the campus community are provided with that policy and acknowledge its receipt, and regularly remind members of the existence of the policy and that their use of campus computers or networks may be monitored. These steps will help limit or negate any due process or privacy claims that may be associated with cases involving free speech or other matters. Both *United States v. Schwartz* (2011), a case involving a Harvard fellow who (before his death) was facing prosecution for distributing copyrighted JSTOR materials, and *United States v. Morris* (1991), which focused on a Cornell University graduate student who created and distributed an Internet worm, provide evidence of the value of such steps.

Kaplin, Lee, Hutchens, and Rooksby (2019, pp. 1091–1092) offer four questions which ought to be considered when constructing acceptable use or other policies for campus computer or network use. Those questions are:

1. Are we seeking to regulate, or do we regulate, the content of computer speech (cyberspeech)?
2. If any of our regulations are content based, do they fit into any First Amendment exceptions that permit content-based regulations—such as the exceptions for obscenity or "true threats"?
3. Does our institution own or lease the computer hardware or software being used for the computer speech; if so, has our institution created "forums" for discussion on its computer servers and networks?
4. Are our regulations or proposed regulations clear, specific, and narrow?

If a proposed or extant policy restricts content that is not in a category of exception from free speech, then any legal challenge to that policy would be conducted using the strict scrutiny standard. Strict scrutiny requires that a policy have both a compelling institutional interest and that it be narrowly tailored. Institutions will be on stronger legal ground when crafting or revising policy if they are not restricting access or use of a public forum (see Chapter 3).

Higher education institutions are well advised to follow the advice of the American Association of University Professors (AAUP) when considering policies that may have an impact on the speech rights of faculty. In 2014 the group affirmed a position it originally took in a 2004 statement:

> Academic freedom, free inquiry, and freedom of expression within the academic community may be limited to no greater extent in electronic format than they are in print, save for the most unusual situation where the very nature of the medium itself might warrant unusual restrictions—and even then only to the extent that such differences demand exceptions or variations.
>
> (p. 1)

Policies aligning with this guidance will also follow the courts' tendency to treat speech concerns in digital communication largely as they have speech concerns in other media.

Recall from Chapter 3 that there is a bit of a paradox when it comes to free speech in higher education relative to curricular and co-curricular arenas. The closer the speech is to the curricular core, the greater the courts expectations have been relative to free speech being protected but the greater the latitude the courts have given to institutions when there is evidence that the college or university has balanced its educational mission with its obligations to protect the rights of the members of the campus community. Sun, Hutchens, and Breslin (2013) discuss this specifically as it relates to online speech.

Kaplin, Lee, Hutchens, and Rooksby (2019) present two more suggestions to help reduce liability for infringing on speech. Treat student cyberspaces (web sites and blogs, for example) like you do the student newspaper (see Chapter 3). Forgo oversight and regulation to the extent that students are not then seen as being agents of the institution. Also, consider working with students and other campus constituents to develop a cyberspace code of ethics to be enforced by peer pressure and counterspeech. Institutions may also consider developing conflict resolution mechanisms related specifically to situations arising from digital communication.

Moving to a more broad recommendation, there may be notable value in campus leaders (students, staff, and faculty) being present in digital communication in ways that help shape the institution's digital communication culture. There may be an understandable hesitancy to engage in an

environment which some consider fraught with potential highly public pit-
falls. The authors of this book believe that there are far more opportunities
for things to go right than there are for things to go wrong, particularly if
leaders engage intentionally as role models in ways that are consistent with
the educational, ethical, legal, and multicultural values of their institution.
In *Campus Life: In Search of Community*, Ernest Boyer argues that colleges and universities should aspire to be communities that are educationally purposeful, open, just, disciplined, caring, and celebrative (Carnegie
Foundation for the Advancement of Teaching, 1990). We believe the goal
of campus leaders engaging in digital communication ought to be fostering
healthier and more vital campus communities as described by Boyer.

One final word in this chapter. Ben-Porath (2018) discusses the way
in which speech conveyed via digital communication can move rapidly
beyond the audience the author may have had in mind for it. Colleges and
universities can quickly find themselves consumed by what seems like a
significant and overwhelming wave of incoming messages about the situation. Ben-Porath (2018) helpfully reminds us all, while social media has
a democratizing potential, it also tends to create echo chambers for like-
minded individuals. These inwardly-reinforcing groups are a function of
friending, liking, and the algorithms which undergird the social media
platforms. Driven by these functions and by the dynamics of in-group
and out-group interactions (Tajfel & Turner, 1979), the rhetoric ramps
up pretty quickly. In developing healthy and helpful responses consistent
with institutional values of inclusion and support for free speech and other
rights, colleges and universities will benefit from being aware of the tyr-
anny of the few. Listen to everyone, but invest the balance of energy and
time in speaking to the larger audiences who may not have already come
to a determined and finite conclusion. Finding those with whom you can
build community and consensus through communication, including digital
communication, may be the most promising pathway for moving forward.

REFERENCES

American Association of University Professors (2014). *Academic freedom and
electronic communications*. Washington, DC: Authors. Retrieved from www.
aaup.org/file/Academic%20Freedom%20%26%20Electronic%20
Communications.pdf

Ben-Porath, S. (2018, October 12). *"LOL I will never be fired": Campus free
speech in the era of social media*. Retrieved from www.law.berkeley.edu/
wp-content/uploads/2018/10/LOL-I-will-never-be-fired.pdf

Berman, A. E., & Dorrier, J. (2016, March 2). Technology feels like it's accelerating:
Because it actually is. *Singularity Hub*. Retrieved from https://singularityhub.

com/2016/03/22/technology-feels-like-its-accelerating-because-it-actually-is/
#sm.001aruqcq10hrfm2115tq5xftfnjj

Browning, J. (2012, December). Universities monitoring the social media accounts of their student-athletes: A recipe for disaster. *Texas Bar Journal, 75*(11), 840–843.

Carnegie Foundation for the Advancement of Teaching (1990). *Campus life: In search of community.* Lawrenceville, NJ: Princeton University Press.

Carr, C. T., & Hayes, R. A. (2015). Social media: Defining, developing and divining. *Atlantic Journal of Communication, 23*(1), 46–65.

Chemerinsky, E., & Gillman, H. (2017). *Free speech on campus.* New Haven, CT: Yale University Press.

Communications Decency Act of 1996 (Title V of the Telecommunications Act of 1996), 47 U.S.C. §223 (2019).

Computer Fraud and Abuse Act (18 U.S.C. § 1030(a)(5)(A)(ii)-(iii) (2019).

Digital Millennium Copyright Act of 1998 17 U.S.C. § 1201 et seq. (2019).

Feminist Majority Foundation v. Hurley, 911 F.3d 674 (4th Cir.).

Florimbio, A. R., Brem, M. J., Garner, A. R., Grigorian, H. L., & Stuart, G. L. (2018). Alcohol-related sex expectancies explain the relation between alcohol use and sexting among college students. *Computers and Human Behavior, 88*, 205–209.

Gajanan, M. (2018, January 18). "I feel horrible": Former University of Alabama student apologizes after using racial slur in video. *Time.* Retrieved from http://time.com/5107228/harley-barber-alabama-racist-video/

Gallup (2018). *Free expression on campus: What college students think about first amendment issues.* Washington, DC: Gallup.

Garcetti v. Ceballos, 547 US 410 (2006).

Gardner, L. (2015, November 13). U. of Illinois settles Salaita case, but will that help it move on? *The Chronicle of Higher Education.* Retrieved from www.chronicle.com/article/U-of-Illinois-Settles-the/234187

Google Spain SL, Google Inc v Agencia Española de Protección de Datos, Mario Costeja González (2014).

Griffin, P. (2017, April 24). The rate of technological change is now exceeding our ability to adapt. *Noted.* Retrieved from www.noted.co.nz/tech/the-rate-of-technological-change-is-now-exceeding-our-ability-to-adapt/

Griwsold v. Connecticut, 381 U.S. 479 (1965).

Higher Education Opportunity Act of 2008, 20 U.S.C. §§ 1092 et seq. (2019).

Ingram, L. A., Macauda, M., Lauckner, C., & Robillard, A. (2019). Sexual behavior, mobile technology use, and sexting among college students in the American south. *American Journal of Health Promotion, 33*(1), 87–96.

Jaschik, S. (2018, December 20). Redefining the obligation to protect students. *Inside Higher Ed*. Retrieved from www.insidehighered.com/news/2018/12/20/court-revives-lawsuit-over-online-threats-made-feminist-students-u-mary-washington

Jones, S., Johnson-Yale, C., Millermaier, S., & Seoane Pérez, F. (2009). Everyday life online: U.S. college students' use of the Internet. *First Monday*, 14(10). Retrieved from https://journals.uic.edu/ojs/index.php/fm/article/view/2649/2301

Kaplin, W. A., Lee, B. A., Hutchens, N. H., & Rooksby, J. H. (2019). *The law of higher education* (6th ed.). San Francisco: Jossey-Bass.

Keefe v. Adams, 840 F.3d 5213 (8th Cir. 2016).

Keyishian v. Board of Regents, 385 U.S. 589 (1967).

Koeppel v. Romano et al., 252 F. Supp.3d 1310 (M.D. Fla. 2017).

Mangan, K. (2018b, April 12). Seething racial tensions prompt sit-in at Texas State U. student center. *The Chronicle of Higher Education*. Retrieved from www.chronicle.com/article/Seething-Racial-Tensions/243109

Marvin, R. (2018, June 13). Charting the rise and fall of teen social media popularity. *PCMag*. Retrieved from www.pcmag.com/news/361755/charting-the-rise-and-fall-of-teen-social-media-popularity

Marvin, R. (2019, April 12). How teen and adult social media usage has (and hasn't) changed. *PCMag*. Retrieved from www.pcmag.com/news/367733/how-teen-and-adult-social-media-usage-has-and-hasnt-chang?utm_source=recirc&utm_medium=news-bottom&utm_campaign=bb1

McAdams v. Marquette University, 914 N.W.2d 708 (Wis. 2018).

Nott, L. (2017, March 14). *Social media speech*. Washington, DC: Freedom Forum Institute. Retrieved from www.freedomforuminstitute.org/first-amendment-center/topics/freedom-of-speech-2/free-speech-on-public-college-campuses-overview/social-media-speech/

Packingham v. North Carolina, 137 S.Ct. 1730 (2017).

Pew Research Center (2018, March 1). *Social media use in 2018*. Washington, DC: Author. Retrieved from www.pewinternet.org/2018/03/01/social-media-use-in-2018/

Pickering v. Board of Education, 391 U.S. 563 (1968).

Privacy Protection Act of 1980 42 U.S.C. §§ 2000aa et seq. (2019).

Raths, D. (2018, May 24). What GDPR means for U.S. higher education. *Campus Technology*. Retrieved from https://campustechnology.com/articles/2018/05/24/what-gdpr-means-for-us-higher-education.aspx

Reyns, B. W., Henson, B., & Fisher, B. S. (2014). Deviance: Low self-control and opportunity as explanations of sexting among college students. *Sociological Spectrum*, 34(3), 273–292.

Right to be forgotten (n.d.). *Intersoft consulting*. Retrieved from https://gdpr-info. eu/issues/right-to-be-forgotten/

Robinson, C. (2018, January 17). Haley Barber apologizes for racist video, says she was expelled from University of Alabama. *Birmingham Real-Time News*. Retrieved from www.al.com/news/birmingham/2018/01/harley_barber_ apologizes_for_r.html

Shelton v. Tucker, 364 U.S. 479 (1960).

Snyder, E., Hutchens, N. H., Jones, W., & Sun, J. C. (2015). Social media policies in intercollegiate athletics: The speech and privacy rights of student-athletes. *Journal for the Study of Sports and Athletes in Education*, 9(1), 50–74.

State v. Drahota, 788 N.W.2d 796 (Neb. 2010).

Sun, J. C., Hutchens, N. H., & Breslin, J. D. (2013). A (virtual) land of confusion with college students' online speech: Introducing the curricular nexus test. *University of Pennsylvania Journal of Constitutional Law*, 16(1), 49–96.

Sweezy v. New Hampshire, 354 U.S. 234 (1957).

Tajfel, H., & Turner, J. C. (1979). An integrative theory of intergroup conflict. In W. G. Austin & S. Worchel (Eds.), *The social psychology of intergroup relations* (pp. 33–47). Monterey, CA: Brooks and Cole Publishing Co.

Tatro v. University of Minnesota, 800 N.W.2d 811 (Minn. App. Ct. 2011).

Tatro v. University of Minnesota, 816 N.W.2d 509 (Minn. 2012).

TEACH Act of 2002 17 U.S.C. §§ et seq. (2019).

Thamel, P. (2012, March 30). Tracking twitter, raising red flags. *New York Times*. Retrieved from www.nytimes.com/2012/03/31/sports/universities-track- athletes-online-raising-legal-concerns.html

Title IX of Education Amendments of 1972 20 U.S.C. §§ 1681 et seq. (2019).

Title VI of The Civil Rights Act of 1964, 42 U.S.C. §§ 2000d et seq. (2019).

Title VII of The Civil Rights Act of 1964, 42 U.S.C. §§ 2001e et seq. (2019).

United States v. Heckenkamp, 482 F.3d (9th Cir. 2007).

United States v. Morris, 928 F.2d 504 (2d Cir. 1991).

United States v. Schwartz, Civ. No. 1:11-cr-10260-NMG (D. Mass. 2011).

United States v. Soderstrand, 412 F.3d 1146 (10th Cir. 2005).

Yeasin v. University of Kansas, 360 P. 3d 423 (Kan. Ct. App. 2015).

Chapter Five

Beyond the Campus
Public Policy and Influencing Organizations

Dean of Students Jacqueline Harris had to make a decision, and none of the options was great. The long-standing dean of students at the state's land grant university was caught between two conservative alumni, one who serves on the state senate and the other who serves on the state assembly. Each is considering sponsorship of a different bill that provides guidance to the state's colleges and universities over free speech rights, and both seek support from the state flagship university. State Senator Elliot Berg is forwarding the model legislation from the Goldwater Institute, and State Assemblyperson Gina Walters is pushing forward with the Forming Open and Robust University Minds (FORUM) Act. Meanwhile, the governor is displeased with the brainwashing, political correctness that her nephew is enduring as a social work student at the flagship university. She wants to encourage her party's senators to introduce a Religious Liberty and Conscience Protection legislation, which would exempt students in certain clinically based, professional programs from engaging in counseling sessions that would conflict with the student's sincerely held religious belief. In light of these three emerging bills, what would you advise your legislators, academic units, and college leadership to consider about these bills?

The narrative in some policy circles is that higher education is unable to respect free speech, particularly conservative ideologies. Higher education is perceived as too politically correct, soft and coddling of its students as well as a bit pushy on the diversity and inclusion agenda. By some accounts, when it comes to free speech policies and practices, higher education is in a state of crisis.

Responding to the posited crisis, some policymakers and influential advocacy groups have swept in as an effort to right-course the perceived problems. For instance, when a handful of law schools (e.g., Southern Illinois University, University of California Hastings College of Law, and

University of Montana) were sued for requiring all students an opportunity to participate in, and in some cases lead, the Christian Legal Society (CLS) chapters on their campuses, the law students sued on First Amendment grounds of speech and religion. Two of the cases (Christian Legal Society v. Walker, 2006; Christian Legal Society v. Kane, 2009) made it to the federal appellate level, and with nearly identical facts, each court decided the cases differently. The case over the CLS chapter at Southern Illinois ruled in favor of the student group to explore the possibility of First Amendment violations. That court concluded that CLS may qualify as an expressive association, so the university's policy improperly interferes with that association's speech by "induc[ing] CLS to alter its membership standards—not merely to allow attendance by nonmembers—in order to maintain recognition" and that would "impair [CLS's] ability to express disapproval of active homosexuality" (p. 863). The case over the CLS chapter at University of California Hastings concluded the opposite, finding that registered student organizations represented a limited public forum and the nondiscrimination policy was a reasonable policy that the university could make. The Hastings case moved up the federal courts, and the U.S. Supreme Court concluded in a 5–4 decision that an all-comers policy, which serves as a viewpoint neutral, nondiscrimination policy for registered student organizations, did not violate the First Amendment and was permissible (Christian Legal Society v. Martinez, 2010).

Many college campuses adopted these nondiscrimination policies, and in light of the U.S. Supreme Court's decision, these other public colleges have a right to enforce their policy. The thought of barring student organizations from forming or de-recognizing them, when their religious or political beliefs are contrary to the nondiscrimination policy, was unsettling to some state legislators. To combat campus adoption of these nondiscrimination policies (also known as all-comers policies), Arizona, Tennessee, and Virginia passed laws allowing registered student organizations, which maintain a religious or political mission, to make membership and leadership decisions without complying to an all-comers policy.

Another example involving a student in a graduate professional program in Michigan is discussed in greater detail later in this chapter. For now, suffice it to say, when policymakers are critical of campus policies that infringe on speech and religion, even with goals to advance diversity and inclusion, the campus policies come under scrutiny. This chapter will examine a series of more recently employed tactics to forward free speech initiatives into our campuses, and we forward analytic approaches to address them including questions to prompt consideration of the policy impacts onto our campuses and messages that the congressional hearings intended to convey as we consider our policies and practices. To those ends, this chapter begins by illustrating how legislation emerges as a reactive policy making approach when legislators are displeased with campus rules or standards of practice, even over curricular matters. While we articulated in Chapter 2 that courts typically defer to curricular and academic learning processes, legislators do not follow that deferential rule so we explain what has happened previously so as to guide the reader on what arguments campus leaders might forward. The chapter also presents the increasing push among states to develop similar policies governing free speech on college campuses, particularly as they apply to public institutions. A small group of advocacy organizations currently is influencing and proposing legislation across the country, and many states have adopted the bills or some variant of them. These bills have a message that disruptors or hecklers of free speech must be controlled and punished, and colleges must take this issue more seriously. Besides reactive and conformity-driven policy approaches, the chapter unveils the investigatory and oversight powers of legislators, specifically Congress, as applied to campus free speech. Four recent congressional hearings are discussed, and we present the themes and our observations of the messages, which the witnesses conveyed to our federal lawmakers as they consider policies in light of the Higher Education Act.

REACTIVE POLICY ENVIRONMENT

Policymakers have reacted to campus efforts that advance diversity and inclusion initiatives by proposing, and sometimes adopting, symbolic legislation—that is to say legislation which has no practical or tangible impact or significance. This is not to say that such legislation is without purpose. First, the symbolic action serves to affirm important ideas, sentiments, or values (Jacobs, 1993; Waldman, 2012; van Klink, 2016). It thus sends a signal of affiliation and affirmation to like-minded individuals (including voting constituents and campaign donors). At the same time, it serves as a line of differentiation with those who are perceived as not sharing those ideas, sentiments, or values. The identification and reification of 'us' and 'them' can be understood as particularly powerful in social phenomena (Tajfel & Turner, 1979). The second purpose served by the symbolic action is to send a message of discomfort and warning (Jacobs, 1993; Waldman, 2012). Just as a rattlesnake's buzzing tail is a reaction to its perception of disruption or threat in its environment, the symbolic legislation conveys both dislike and fair notice that something more may be about to happen if the irritant is not reduced or removed. It is not necessary that symbolic legislation actually be enacted in order for it to achieve these two purposes.

A Case Study

Illustrating this point, recall the circumstances at hand in *Ward v. Polite* (2012) as discussed in Chapter 2. Julea Ward, a graduate counseling student at Eastern Michigan University, requested a referral of a gay client. Her rationale was that her religious values conflicted with homosexuality so she could not counsel the client. Because of those differences, she requested to exercise the referral process. The American Counseling Association's guidelines do not compel a counselor or counseling student in a practicum to adopt the client's beliefs; however, a counselor or counseling student in a practicum is expected to offer support and guidance, "even to clients whose practices one may find distasteful or morally wrong" (Oppenheimer, 2012, p. A18). Ward's professors found her use of the referral process to be inappropriate because it demonstrated an unwillingness to address the client. In light of Ward's action, she was academically disciplined, which eventually led to her academic dismissal from the program. She sued citing free speech violations and religious discrimination. The well-funded Alliance Defense Fund, a conservative Christian, legal advocacy group, took the case.

The trial court ruled in favor of the public university, and the appellate court generally restated many of the same legal policies about professional deference to academic judgments over curriculum and learning processes. The appellate court did question some of the interactions and reasoning behind Eastern Michigan University's decision to dismiss Ward, and that court sent the case back to the trial court to dig deeper into the case facts to see if there was any pretext based on religious discrimination. As stated in Chapter 2, counseling professors at Eastern Michigan University testified in rather peculiarly ways raising points such as: Did Julea Ward believe that "'anyone [is] more righteous than another before God?' and whether, if Ward's stated beliefs were true, 'doesn't that mean that you're all on the same boat and shouldn't [gays and lesbians] be accorded the same respect and honor that God would give them?'" (p. 738).

Rather than continuing the case, the parties settled. We never learned what the court might have found upon a second review, which would have consisted of an investigation as to whether religious discrimination took place. This inquiry would have been particularly instructive to provide more legal guidance on the line between the speech rights associated with the academic program to design curriculum and instruct in ways fulfilling the requisite rule of legitimate pedagogical concern and meeting the professional standards, on the one hand, and the free exercise rights of the student in a professional program to assert a referral when a client's values and personal life conflict with the student's values and personal life, on the other hand.

Lawmakers' Reaction to the College Policy and Court Case

Although the court did not speak further on this matter because of the settled case, the Michigan legislature voiced its opposition to Eastern Michigan University's academic judgment. The Michigan Senate forwarded a resolution (Michigan Senate Resolution No. 66, 2011) seeking the "[U.S.] President and the United States Congress to enact legislation protecting the rights of conscience of students seeking counseling degrees and licensed professional counselors." While no federal legislative action emerged from that resolution, both the Michigan Senate and House responded in June and October 2011, respectively. Drawing on their legislative powers, each legislative chamber crafted and forwarded a symbolic legislative bill. The Michigan Senate forwarded Senate Bill 518, and the Michigan House forwarded House Bill 5040. Both bills were dedicated to Julea Ward and contained nearly identical language. Each chamber made it loud and clear that each objected to the treatment of Julea Ward for the university's discriminatory practice by not allowing her to conscientiously object to counseling a gay client, through a counseling referral, based on her religious beliefs. To that end, each bill's preamble made clear that the bill's purpose was "to protect the right of a student to assert conscientious objection to providing certain counseling or other services; to prohibit certain actions by institutions of higher education; and to provide remedies" (Julea Ward Freedom of Conscience Act, 2011, 2012). In the primary provision of the bills each outlined the prohibited discriminatory treatment stating:

> A public degree or certificate granting college, university, junior college, or community college of this state shall not discipline or discriminate against a student in a counseling, social work, or psychology program because the student refuses to counsel or serve a client as to goals, outcomes, or behaviors that conflict with a sincerely held religious belief of the student, if the student refers the client to a counselor who will provide the counseling or services.
>
> (Julea Ward Freedom of Conscience Act, 2011,
> S.B. 518 Section 3; 2012 H.B. 5040 Section 3)

The Senate bill included application to both public and private postsecondary educational institutions, but the House bill only pertained to public colleges and universities.

The Senate bill failed to move forward, but in June 2012, the House bill passed 59–50. Neither bill was enacted into law, but collectively, they conveyed a loud message that professional associations and higher education professional education programs could, in the future, be subject to penalties when one of these entities fails to appropriately accommodate religious freedoms.

Implications of the Proposed Bills

As noted in Chapter 2 of this book, helping professions, which include counseling, social work, and psychology, have professional standards that consider client-centered perspectives. The intent of these professional standards is not to compel a professional in the field to change their ideology or their personal lives, but instead, the professional standards are written to avoid discriminatory treatment, promote inclusive services, and understand the perspectives in which the client takes in order to provide better services. Consider the practical implications arising from the Ward case. Julea Ward intended to serve as a school counselor. As American Civil Liberties Union (ACLU) attorney Daniel Mach, who in his capacity at the ACLU filed a brief in support of Eastern Michigan University, asserted in an interview with the *New York Times*, "Nobody should be forced to change her religious beliefs or be punished for her faith" (Oppenheimer, 2012, p. A18). The situation with Ward's decision moves beyond that point. Referring a client is not a neutral act and may have consequences. Julea Ward expressed in the court case that she sought this degree to consider serving as a high school counselor after having taught previously at the high school level. This professional preparation is even more for Ward, as Mach explains, "high school counselors may be the only compassionate adults available to gay, bisexual or transgender youths, and that turning away such a youth in crisis [as Ward did in this case] 'could be devastating.'" (Oppenheimer, 2012, p. A18). The professional standard is intended to combat the potentially significant and adverse impacts on the student, but these proposed laws could make conscientious objection a legitimate reason to turn away an individual in need.

The National Association of Social Workers and the Michigan Chapter of the National Association of Social Workers (2011) submitted a joint statement opposing Senate Bill 518 and House Bill 5040. Referencing their Code of Ethics as a professional standard, they expressed problems with the legislative bills as extending beyond religious freedom.

> The social work profession has not condoned conduct in which the social worker selects clients or provides treatment based on negative thoughts or beliefs about a class of persons who have immutable characteristics, such as their race, color, or national origin.
>
> (p. 2)

These bills would counter the profession's ethical code by granting social workers greater independence on whom they served presenting potential discriminatory or simply unjust practices and underrepresentation for certain groups. The authors of the joint statement emphasized that one of the purposes of this ethical code was to ensure that social workers and students of the profession "gain competency in understanding and treating diverse populations in the larger society" (p. 2). These arguments were also echoed by the Presidents' Council for the State Universities of Michigan when Michael Boulus (2012b), the association's executive director, testified at the hearing that the students must both understand and apply the lessons and code of ethics.

In the House Education Committee hearing for the Julea Ward Freedom of Conscience Act, Dr. Judith Kovach, a licensed psychologist and a policy consultant for the Michigan Psychological Association, reiterated the prior concerns about the legislative bill's conflict with the three named professions' code of ethics and the legislative impact on social justice and multicultural inclusion. She also presented three other concerns. First, she pointed out how the House bill interferes with academic freedom. The faculty for the professional programs establish the knowledge and skills that students must meet, but this legislation circumvents the curricular decision-making. She asserts that the "intrusion of state legislatures into the education and training of mental health professionals is very troubling" because there is "no justification for this action" especially when there are regulatory bodies, such as the Board of Psychology, in place. Further, this bill presents a slippery slope where more governmental intrusion may become more normative than it should. Second, this bill undermines national accreditation standards. Accreditation represents a peer review process with existing established standards and checks. This bill would disregard the peer review process. Finally, Dr. Kovach warns that "the most egregious aspect of HB 5040 is the potential disregard for the public welfare" (Julea Ward Freedom of Conscience Act, 2012a, p. 2). Although the current professional standards require preparing students as future professionals with a "wide variety of clients without harming them," the under or selective preparation presents the "potential to allow great harm to the citizens of Michigan" through this state legislation (Julea Ward Freedom of Conscience Act, 2012, p. 3).

The bill sends a message that the helping professions—counseling, psychology, and social work—are "soft" fields that have fungible and disposable standards. Further, this bill may open the gate for other bills that restrict or dictate what professional standards must be in place for these fields as well as other fields. Those bills would alter the balance between a profession's right to shape and guard its practice.

Still Pending

The Julea Ward Freedom of Conscience Act is part of the Religious Liberty and Conscience Protection Act, which, at the time of this publication, are still proposed bills. Because of a significant base of protectionists for religious freedom, which for all intents and purposes represents protections over Christianity, the bill continues to emerge in Michigan.

Michigan was not the only state to tackle the perceived professional and academic intrusion onto religious rights. Other states, for example Arizona and Tennessee, have proposed conscience and refusal clauses within their religion liberty bills. In Arizona, an education bill, Arizona H.B. 2565, was signed into law under a state provision granting "[r]ights of students at universities and community colleges" (Amending Title 15, 2011). The pertinent excerpt states:

> A university or community college shall not discipline or discriminate against a student in a counseling, social work or psychology program because the student refuses to counsel a client about goals that conflict with the student's sincerely held religious belief if the student consults with the supervising instructor or professor to determine the proper course of action to avoid harm to the client.
>
> (Amending Title 15, 2011)

Today, that language is incorporated into law within the Arizona Revised Statutes as provisions "Relating to Universities and Community Colleges."

Bills, like the one in Michigan, and the law in Arizona are not likely going away. Legislation around the conscience clause movement is likely to emerge as the consciousness for LGBTQ equity increases; these legislative responses will likely creep up as we saw in legislative battle ground for gender inclusive bathrooms and other educational access (Lewis, Fetter-Harrott, Sun, & Eckes, 2017).

CONFORMITY POLICY ENVIRONMENT

In the area of free speech and inclusive campuses, several advocacy groups have served as watchdogs over higher education free speech policies and practices. Further, they have influenced policymakers to propose legislation or adopt new state laws that add protections over free speech in new ways such as creating complainant rights in an analogous manner to campus sexual harassment policies and protocols. Based on policies they propose and actions that they have taken and are described below, the goal of these advocacy groups appears to be disseminating a set of rules and practices by proliferating, in an organized and systematic manner, legislation and judicial decisions that create conformity of their policy agenda. In other words, they wish to create the bills that become legislation and tackle the cases that set precedence, and these sources of law will create conformance.

Advocacy Groups

Many professional organizations and advocacy groups influence campus free speech laws and policies. Three are most directly involved in the shaping of laws, policies, and other measures when matters of diversity and inclusion are at issue.

The Alliance Defending Freedom (ADF) has increasingly taken interest in college free speech policies conflicting with religious freedoms. ADF is often characterized as a nonprofit, conservative Christian organization that founded to "reverse the growing threat to religious freedom." Today, it serves as a watchdog over college intrusions into religious beliefs, particularly Christianity. ADF is well staffed with attorneys. It "has more than 3,000 lawyers working on behalf of its causes around the world and brought in $51.5 million in revenue for the 2015–16 tax year, more than the American Civil Liberties Union" (Peters, 2017, p. A1). In late 2016, it had been actively engaged with lawsuits "in California, Iowa, Wisconsin, and Michigan against universities that are favoring certain viewpoints over others and silencing free speech on campus" (Kramer, 2016). By the words of the organization itself, "it doesn't appear to be slowing down" over its quest to correct alleged wrongdoing by colleges that restrict religious freedoms (Kramer, 2016).

The Foundation for Individual Rights in Education (FIRE) has been protecting the civil liberties of college students and faculty for over 20 years, often issuing letters and notices that a college is violating or presents a policy potentially in violation of the First Amendment, particularly with respect to the free speech clause, or Fourteenth Amendment, due process clause. FIRE is a non-profit civil liberties organization that defends the rights of college students and postsecondary faculty. The legal areas of interest include "freedom of speech, freedom of association, due process, legal equality, religious liberty, and sanctity of conscience." FIRE's work with higher education institutions often falls within four categories—education and training of higher education professionals, college policy crafting and evaluations (e.g., scoring of speech codes), legislation, and litigation. To those ends, "FIRE defends those whose rights are denied on campus, regardless of identity or viewpoint, and we educate those on and off campus about these rights and their importance." FIRE's role in education and policy-making impact many colleges on a regular basis because of their speech code status. Notably, "[o]f the 466 schools reviewed by FIRE, 133, or 28.5%, received a red light rating. 285 schools received a yellow light rating (61.2%), and 42 received a green light rating (9%). Six schools earned a Warning rating (1.5%)" (Foundation for Individual Rights in Education, 2019). From 2009 to 2019, FIRE reports that the number of red light colleges declined by nearly 45 percentage points. In other words, the organization reports significant gains in its ability to change college policies to conform with First Amendment law and free speech principles.

The third association, the Goldwater Institute, drew attention more significantly around 2015 as states began to wrestle with their relevant statutes. In fact, many legislative bills on campus free speech likely have the imprint and language derived from the Goldwater Institute. Considered a think tank, the Goldwater Institute is a politically conservative organization with libertarian views on free speech. It is named after Barry Goldwater, Arizona's five-term Republican senator, who cared deeply about individual liberties. The Goldwater Institute advocates for states to adopt its legislative model for campus free speech rules (Kurtz, Manley, & Butcher, 2017; Peters, 2017, 2018). In addition, it actively engages in lawsuits against colleges that interfere with speech rights as individual liberties.

State Laws

Policymakers have increasingly taken interest in state law changes governing civil liberties as the source to grant greater free speech on college campuses. The American Legislative Exchange Council (ALEC), which works with state legislators to promote aggressively conservative policies, has been aligned with the Goldwater Institute as well as advancing a variant to that proposed bill under the Forming Open and Robust University Minds Act and the Campus Free Expression Act. The contributions to each law are listed below along with sample states that have passed the legislation.

Goldwater Institute

According to the Goldwater Institute, the model bill incorporates the following provisions (Kurtz, Manley, & Butcher, 2017, p. 2):

- It creates an official university policy that strongly affirms the importance of free expression, nullifying any existing restrictive speech codes in the process.
- It prevents administrators from disinviting speakers, no matter how controversial, whom members of the campus community wish to hear from.

120

- It establishes a system of disciplinary sanctions for students and anyone else who interferes with the free speech rights of others.
- It allows persons whose free speech rights have been improperly infringed by the university to recover court costs and attorney's fees.
- It reaffirms the principle that universities, at the official institutional level, ought to remain neutral on issues of public controversy to encourage the widest possible range of opinion and dialogue within the university itself.
- It ensures that students will be informed of the official policy on free expression.
- It authorizes a special subcommittee of the university board of trustees to issue a yearly report to the public, the trustees, the governor, and the legislature on the administrative handling of free speech issues.

The authors of the report emphasize that "[s]tudents will know from the moment they enter the university that they must respect the free expression of others, and will face significant consequences if they do not" (Kurtz, Manley, & Butcher, 2017, p. 5).

Resembling somewhat the 2011 Dear Colleague Letter governing Title IX peer sexual assault guidelines for campuses, the comprehensive nature of the model legislation presents more avenues to ensure free speech rights are respected with direct mandates and oversight. In more practical terms for campus leaders, the model legislation prohibits public colleges from disinviting speakers mandating issue neutrality on matters of public controversy. The model legislation also establishes penalties, especially for those individuals who interfered more than once. A provision within the model language permits a right to sue and attorneys' fees if an individual has had one's speech disrupted or blocked from exercising free speech. Adding protections, the model language mandates public colleges to establish a "Committee on Free Expression," which serves as an oversight committee. A provision also provides oversight responsibilities including an annual reporting requirement. Embedded in the language, regular training and communication are required to new students, faculty, and staff about their free speech rights pursuant to the law. States such as Arizona (Arizona Amending Sections 15-1861 and 15-1864, 2016; Arizona Amending Sections 13-2906, 15-1861 and 15-1864, 2016), Georgia (Campus Free Speech Act, 2018), and North Carolina (Restore/Preserve Campus Free Speech Act, 2017) have Goldwater-inspired laws in place.

Forming Open and Robust University Minds (FORUM) Act

With the support of the American Legislative Executive Council (ALEC), a conservative association connected with business interests, several states have adopted or entertained an alternative model legislation, Forming Open and Robust University Minds (FORUM) Act. According to ALEC (2018),

> This model policy applies to public institution of higher education and does the following: A) eliminates "free speech zones;" B) protects the right of all people to engage in lawful expression; C) protects students and student groups from disciplinary action because of their lawful expression, including belief-based organizations; D) requires that students be educated regarding their free speech rights/responsibilities; E) requires that administrators, campus police, etc. understand their duties regarding free expression on campus; and F) most importantly, empowers legislators to hold universities accountable by requiring each institution to report on free speech issues prior to the legislature's appropriations process; G) allows alleged victims to bring a cause of action for violation of their free speech rights.
>
> (para. 1)

States that have enacted legislation inspired by the ALEC FORUM Act include Arkansas (Forming Open and Robust University Minds Act, 2019), Kentucky (Campus Free Speech Protection Act, 2019), and Tennessee (Campus Free Speech Protection Act, 2017).

Campus Free Expression (CAFE) Act

While the FORUM Act eliminates free speech zones, proposed legislation by the Foundation for Individual Rights in Education (FIRE)—the Campus Free Expression (CAFE) Act—eliminates the campus free speech limits through free speech zones, and it transforms a campus so the outdoor areas are considered viable spaces for free speech. According to FIRE (2015),

> CAFE is legislation designed to prohibit public colleges and universities from limiting speech and expressive activity to unconstitutionally restrictive "free speech zones." These "zones" are maintained by hundreds of public colleges and universities nationwide and restrict students' First Amendment rights. Under CAFE, the open, outdoor

areas of public campuses would be presumed available for students to exercise their free speech rights, subject only to the reasonable limitations.

(para. 1)

Under the CAFE Act, campuses may still maintain reasonable rules around time, place, and manner, and they are permissible policies, "so long as those rules are content and viewpoint-neutral, further one of the school's significant interests, and leave ample alternatives for students to engage in expressive activity." Similarly, expressions that disrupt learning would be located elsewhere on the campus.

States that have laws inspired by the CAFE Act include Colorado (Students' Right to Speak in a Public Forum), Florida (Campus Free Expression Act), Missouri (Campus Free Expression Act), Utah (Campus Free Expression Act), and Virginia (Campus Free Expression Act).

State Law Analysis

Campus leaders should take note of the laws and policies applicable to one's state. Campus leaders should review the law considering the following question prompts to uncover the implications and check for alignment between the law and the school policy:

- Who is subject to the free speech law? Are outside agitators and members of the campus community treated differently, and if so, in what ways?
- How does the law treat disinvitations? Does it restrict such a practice?
- How does the law define or treat free speech zones? Are all outer areas presumptively free speech zones?
- What are the limits or conditions to placing reasonable restrictions to spaces designated for free speech?
- What are the reporting guidelines about free speech matters? What are the criteria and timeline, and who are the responsible parties for remedying and reporting any violations or flags?
- Is there a mandated body, which reviews data and assesses the campus climate? What are the expectations, and how are these roles different from other data reporting and assessment activities such as under Clery, Title IX, and other reports?
- How does the policy impact existing student conduct and registered student organization policies (e.g., all-comers policy for student organization membership)?

- What type of notice, hearing, and appeal criteria and practice standards are in place for students who complain of intellectual discrimination or other free speech matters?

A peer institution at another state may have conducted a similar analysis. That analysis may be helpful as a guide; however, even when a law is inspired by model legislation from a group, the law often morphs into its own provisions and presents significantly different language throughout the text. Further, a peer institution may reside in a state that cross-lists legislative mandates. For instance, in Arizona, the laws relating to public assembly are applicable to postsecondary institutions, whereas, Colorado law is fairly tight so its legislative applications within postsecondary education is largely covered within that states' statutory chapter for postsecondary education. Given these differences among states, a joint effort to analyze the law among the institutions within the state may, in the long-run, be the best source to dissect the effects of the law. Also, a conversation with the state's Legislative Service Commission or Legislative Research Commission, often a nonpartisan agency that supports bill drafting and analysis, may be fruitful to understanding the legislative intent and implementation considerations.

INVESTIGATORY POLICY ENVIRONMENT

Policymakers have investigatory powers. Congress has used that power and has intended to send a strong message to reform campus free speech practices, which some claim is in a state of crisis. Given the perceived crisis, both chambers drew on the opportunity of the pending Higher Education Act Reauthorization and oversight authority as avenues to convey a message that campuses should quiet the commotion created from protests—depicted in the media as out of control and unsafe and closed minded and unaccepting of counter viewpoints. Four congressional hearings, which are described below, took place between 2017 and 2018.

Free Speech 101: The Assault on the First Amendment on College Campuses

On June 20, 2017, the Senate Committee on the Judiciary held a hearing on Free Speech 101: The Assault on the First Amendment on College Campuses. The inquiry unveiled questions such as how have colleges blocked individuals from speaking on campuses, what legal rules should campus leaders follow, and what changes might be entertained to overcome the current obstacles to free speech on college campuses? (Larimer, 2017).

Seven witnesses, who had a diverse set of experiences with campus free speech issues, testified. The cast of experts included two students who experienced free speech challenges—one at a private college and one at a public college—a former university president who also serves as a senior scholar at Yale Law, a vice president of campus life of American University, a senior scholar of First Amendment at UCLA School of Law, president of the Southern Poverty Law Center, and a notable First Amendment attorney.

The more than two hours of testimony spurred a series of criticisms about higher education's handling of free speech on potentially offensive matters about race and sexual harassment. Zachery Wood, a student from the private school, Williams College, testified depicting a situation when private college leadership cancelled John Derbyshire's address without offering the campus an opportunity to engage in intellectual debate. Derbyshire was a former writer for the *National Review*. He was fired after posting a blog on *Taki's Magazine* titled, The Talk: The Nonblack Version (Derbyshire, 2012). Derbyshire presented a series of negative statements depicting persons who are Black as dangerous and undesirable associates. For instance, he wrote that a default rule is to treat persons who are Black with the "same courtesies," then he proceeded to explain "this default principle should be overridden by considerations of personal safety" with no regard that this principle, if held, would equally apply to other racial groups (Derbyshire, 2012, para. 9). Derbyshire (2012) also wrote a listing of deplorables including, "Avoid concentrations of blacks not all known to you personally" (para. 16) and, "If planning a trip to a beach or amusement park at some date, find out whether it is likely to be swamped with blacks on that date (neglect of that one got me the closest I have ever gotten to death by gunshot)" (para. 18). These statements and others, which present expressions of hatred and advocate for social separation, occurred during the Black Lives Matter movement and a series of inadvertent shootings of Black males that led to deaths. The president of the private college reviewed Derbyshire's writing and concluded that the "understanding I came to of [Derbyshire's] writing was that it was simply racist ranting, with no redeeming intellectual value whatsoever" (Svrluga, 2016, para. 7). Failing to see the redeeming value, he reminded the campus community, "The college does not have an obligation to give a platform to absolutely anybody" (Svrluga, 2016, para. 7). Given the college's right to speak and not provide a forum for Derbyshire, the private college president added, "And a self-proclaimed white supremacist who was going to come and tell students . . . that they should avoid the African American students, was over a line" (Svrluga, 2016, para. 7).

Wood, who is Black and self-identified as a Democrat and liberal, was, at the time of the incident, a sophomore at the private college and leader of the Uncomfortable Learning, a student group intended to bring provocative experiences to the otherwise quiet, academically centered Massachusetts campus (Svrluga, 2016). After he invited Derbyshire, Wood encountered a series of negative encounters from his fellow students, not administrators. According to his Senate hearing testimony, he expressed, "I have faced considerable backlash from the student body" (Free Speech 101-Wood, 2017e, para. 5). The event generated emotions on his campus leading to unwelcoming expressions in which he was "a sellout" and "anti-black" with leanings as "a men's rights activist" (Free Speech 101-Wood, 2017e, para. 5). He received more cryptic messages, including anonymous ones, too.

> On Facebook, one student wrote that "they need the oil and the switch to deal with him [me] in this midnight hour." Once, I even received a hand-written letter, slipped under my door, that read: "your blood will be on the leaves."
>
> (Free Speech 101-Wood, 2017e, para. 5)

Ironically, these reactions to Wood's expressions, which were raised to demonstrate insensitivity to free speech, are forms of free speech—the very kind and nature that some legislators and panelist seek to defend, protect, and ensure penalties to those who seek to quash it.

Challenges to Freedom of Speech on College Campuses, Part I

Then on July 27, 2017, a joint subcommittee from the House Committee on Oversight and Government Reform convened the Challenges to Freedom of Speech on College Campuses hearing. According to the House committees' charge, the purpose of the hearing was:

> To identify the harms of infringing on the right to free speech on college campuses; To explore recommendations on how to encourage and protect First Amendment rights, as well as intellectual and ideological diversity, on college campuses.; To understand administrators' concerns about public safety and controversial speakers on campus, which sometimes lead to unconstitutional restrictions on free speech.
>
> (para. 1)

With the intention to better understand the climate on college campuses, propose solutions, and uphold the First Amendment, the committees invited experts whom members of the joint subcommittees characterized as being "at the forefront of this debate" (Challenges to Freedom of Speech, 2017f, para. 2). The congressional committee invited five speakers, who, by their experiences, serve as informants to this issue. The list of speakers included a law professor who previously served as president of the American Civil Liberties Union; Ben Shapiro, one of the provocative campus speakers who encountered hecklers at his talks; a comedian and filmmaker of the documentary, No Safe Spaces, which depicts universities as closed to free speech and characterizes campus safe spaces as emotional shields on college campuses; a former provost and vice president of academic affairs of a private college that encountered tension following a faculty member's public criticism; and a former university president, who served as the Anti-Defamation League representative.

Three hours of testimony and political framing characterized campuses as unhealthy, closed-minded learning spaces (Friedersdorf, 2017; Kinery, 2017). The hearing opened with a 50-second video montage of free speech interferences with public university incidents including students and other spectators shouting down Ben Shapiro at the University of Wisconsin–Madison and the Berkeley riots, which were referenced in Chapter 1, as the reception to Milo Yiannopoulos and led to significant media coverage about the breach of peace with firework rockets lighting up the sky. The video also framed the incidents at private colleges including Milo Yiannopoulos confronted by hecklers who overtook the stage at the Catholic university, DePaul, and Charles Murray who experienced significant disruption from a crowd of students at Middlebury. Following the video, Representative Jim Jordan, the Subcommittee on Healthcare, Benefits and Administrative Rules chair, opened the meeting asserting how the sensitive responses from higher education consist of "trigger warnings, safe spaces, safe zones, shout-downs, microaggressions, [and] bias response teams" have stifled our campuses' ability to further free speech by catering to the disruptors, not the speakers (Challenges to Freedom of Speech-Jordan, 2017a, para 2).

While the legal scholar and former administrators presented practical problems and misunderstandings on college campuses, conservative provocateur Ben Shapiro and comedian and filmmaker Adam Carolla characterized college students as shielded and sensitive beings unprepared for adulthood. Carolla argued, "We're talking a lot about the kids, and I think they're just that, kids" (Challenges to Freedom of Speech-Carolla, 2017b, para. 8). Depicting college students as overly protected, he reminded the members of Congress that college students "grew up dipped in Purell, playing soccer games where they never kept score, and watching Wow! Wow! Wubbzy! and we're asking them to be mature" (para. 8). He asserted that society, especially educators, the "adults who are in charge of these kids," change our practices (para. 11). He analogized,

> You need to expose your children to germs and dirt in the environment to build up their immune system. [Yet, o]ur plan is put them in a bubble, keep them away from everything, and somehow they'll come out stronger when they emerge from the bubble.
>
> (para. 10)

Ben Shapiro (Challenges to Freedom of Speech-Shapiro, 2017c) simplified the situation among dissenters to certain conservative speech. He forwarded the idea that a scripted playbook silences free speech of conservative perspectives.

> Free speech is under assault because of a three step argument made by the advocates and justifiers of violence. The first step is that they say the validity or invalidity of an argument can be judged solely by the ethnic, sexual, racial, or cultural identity of the person making the argument. The second step is that those who argue otherwise are engaging in verbal violence. And the third step is that they conclude physical violence is sometimes justified to stop what they call verbal violence.
>
> (para. 4)

He warns that a person's identity controls social acceptability if one may assert subjective insensitivities or not. Posing a hypothetical, Shapiro stated, "If a straight white male or anybody else who ranks lower on the victimhood scale says something contrary to the viewpoints of the higher-ranking intersectional–intersectionality identity, that person has engaged in a microaggression" (Challenges to Freedom of Speech-Shapiro, 2017c, para. 6). Minimizing the application and effect of microaggression, he added, "You don't have to actively say anything insulting to microaggress. Somebody merely needs to take offense" (para 7).

Although the characterization of college students with hyperbolic messages of their sensitivities likely overstates conditions on campuses, the testimony raised some similar messages from other legislative hearings about maintaining a welcoming campus to free speech, using free speech to counter speech one does not support, and acknowledging that hate speech is not really a *per se* protection within the First Amendment (Friedersdorf, 2017; Kinery, 2017).

Exploring Free Speech on College Campuses

On October 26, 2017, the political spectacle continued and discussions about free speech on college campuses emerged through another congressional committee. The Senate engaged in this discussion, except this time, it was the Senate Committee on Health, Education, Labor, and Pensions which held a hearing titled Exploring Free Speech on College Campuses. Unlike the prior two hearings, the four panelists offered expertise of the University of Chicago president, whose campus has constructed a public statement about respecting free speech as a clear institutional value; a law professor who previously served as president of the American Civil Liberties Union; the president of the Southern Poverty Law Center; and a Middlebury professor, who was the middle of that campus' controversy.

While three of the panelists discussed the law and campus leadership recommendations, Dr. Allison Stanger shared an incident involving her at Middlebury College. Students at Middlebury asked her to moderate a presentation by Edward Snowden and Charles Murray. She recounted, "Snowden's presentation went forward without a problem" (Exploring Free Speech—Stanger, para. 2). By contrast, protestors, primarily students, derailed Murray's attempted presentation. He never spoke, and Murray and Stanger "were forced to retreat to another location to live stream [the] conversation." Stanger noted how Murray and she were "intimidated and physically assaulted" as they tried to exit the auditorium. As recounted in a *New York Times* article, Stanger "suffered a concussion after someone grabbed her hair and twisted her neck" (Saul, 2017, p. A15). According to Stanger, the incident illustrated the role of a small, yet impressionable, group of faculty, who influenced students to behave in a manner that they espoused. Stanger testified that this "small minority of Middlebury faculty . . . cheered on the protests, which is their right," but she also remarked at the uninformed understanding from which some of the faculty operated (Exploring Free Speech—Stanger, para. 5). Stanger (2017) reported how "these faculty . . . did not encourage their students to read Charles Murray or listen to him first before drawing their own conclusions about his work or his character" (para. 5). Equally concerning, Stanger believed that the students believed shutting down Murray's speech furthered social justice. She opined that "some Middlebury professors shared that view, thereby encouraging radical action" (para. 6). At the end, Stanger reiterated that censorship only reflects a very small minority view, and college students are generally accepting and engaged in such dialogue. She described that the campus environment welcomes "a learning environment where ideas can freely collide" (para. 12). She is also not closed to the practical consideration that campus must maintain "some safe enclaves on campus to foster inclusivity" (para. 15).

129

The panelists generally held similar positions. Although Stanger described an event that stood out as an outlier to higher education's free speech environment, the other panelists described campus environments that foster dialogue and debate as part of the learning process. "While senators pressed witnesses for best practices, constitutional requirements to uphold free speech and the balance of liberal and conservative voices on campus, the general consensus was that the colleges themselves were doing their best to uphold the First Amendment" (Roll, 2017b, para. 9). Given the best efforts, the panelists shied away from governmental interventions.

Challenges to Freedom of Speech on College Campuses, Part II

On May 22, 2018, the two subcommittees within the House Committee on Oversight and Government Reform continued their inquiry from July 2017 examining the Challenges to the Freedom of Speech on College Campuses, Part II. The committee representatives consisted of five speakers consisting of the lead attorney and director for the Center for Academic Freedom at the Alliance Defending Freedom; the Middlebury professor, who was the middle of that campus' controversy and presented at a Senate hearing; a former Evergreen State professor, who was the center of a controversy at that campus; a notable social scientist, who founded and directs an interdisciplinary race and equity research center; and a well-regarded legal philosopher, who directs a center on the study of American constitutional issues.

Bret Weinstein, who bestowed onto himself the honorary title of "professor in exile" from Evergreen State College, testified about his encounters with a once annual event, The Day of Absence. For many years at Evergreen State, the symbolic day called for minority students and faculty members to meet off campus and engage in a dialogue about furthering an inclusive campus. The absence of the persons would highlight their significance to the campus, and following the primary portion of the day, a campus unity event would be held to draw multiple members of the community together. The previous hosting of this day drew campus grumblings, but the 2017 event raised contentious clashes when the organizers proposed switching the campus event to have White faculty and staff stay off campus. Professor Weinstein objected, sending a campus email distribution stating in part:

> There is a huge difference between a group or coalition deciding to voluntarily absent themselves from a shared space in order to highlight their vital and underappreciated roles (the theme of the Douglas Turner Ward play *Day of Absence*, as well as the recent

Women's Day walkout), and a group encouraging another group to go away. . . . The first is a forceful call to consciousness, which is, of course, crippling to the logic of oppression. The second is a show of force, and an act of oppression in and of itself.

(Jaschik, 2018, para. 8)

Weinstein sued the college for $3.85 million asserting "hostility based on race" because the college failed to defend his speech, which permitted the harassing and hostile work environment (Roll, 2017a). Weinstein and his wife, who was also a faculty member at Evergreen State, settled with the college and left it for a total sum of $500,000 between the couple (Jaschik, 2018; Roll, 2017a).

According to Weinstein's testimony at the May 2018 House hearing, he was cast away from the Academy and he was subjugated to the "Intellectual Dark Web" (Challenges to Freedom of Speech II, min 43). Disgruntled about the infringements to free speech, he cautions that college campuses are enclaves of closed-minded environments. He asked, "Am I alleging a conspiracy?" Answering in the negative, he posited, "What I have seen functions much more like a cult," and he warned of the power and control leading to a groupthink mindset, which counters the public engagement which he says is lacking in higher education (Challenges to Freedom of Speech II-Weinstein, 2018a, min. 42). Ultimately, Weinstein believes that there is "a threat of crippling stigma and the destruction of their capacity to learn" that will continue until campuses embrace principles of free speech (Challenges to Freedom of Speech II-Weinstein, 2018a, min. 42).

Not all the speakers had such a gloomy outlook as Weinstein over the state of campus free speech. While several speakers deemed the campus free speech rights as in crisis, others believed that the events signal isolated instances. Further, across the board the speakers envisioned solutions heavily drawing on First Amendment principles, not additional legislation.

OBSERVATIONS AND THEMES

After four distinct legislative committees and 21 statements (with four panelists who testified twice making the total at 17 unique perspectives), Congress heard about campuses intervening on free speech, students and other spectators' disruption of speech opportunities, and the legal rules that establish free speech rights. The congressional committees entertained ideas to address what many of these legislators saw as a growing crisis against free speech principles. Across the panels, several observations and themes emerged and they contribute to our understanding about the conflicts between free speech and efforts to further an inclusive campus.

131

Social Institutions With a Special Obligation

Unequivocally, the panelists believed that colleges and universities represent the social institutions obligated to further free speech principles and practices. They upheld free speech as a core value for our campuses. As Frederick Lawrence, the representative for the Anti-Defamation League, noted, American colleges and universities are each distinct is many ways, yet he identified one way in which they are alike. He remarked,

> Most if not all schools share a similar mission—to discover and create knowledge, and to transmit that knowledge through our teaching and our scholarship, for the betterment of our local, national and even international communities. For this mission, free expression and free inquiry are essential.
>
> (Free Speech 101-Lawrence, 2017f, para. 12)

To that end, Senator Tim Kaine expressed in one of the hearings,

> Colleges should be a place of robust speech and disagreement. We don't need to protect people from free speech; we need to expose them to different ideas and have them use their critical faculties to determine what is right and wrong.
>
> (Free Speech 101-Caine, 2017b, para. 1)

Further, while the legal scholars presented distinctions about free speech based on First Amendment law and private colleges' practice as potentially a contractual obligation, the legislators and panelists were generally referencing free speech as a principled obligation making the public/private distinction nearly non-existent because free speech is simply a core value of the social institution. Even with the law, Professor Volokh of UCLA argued that "if leading private universities suppress dissenting viewpoints, that too is bad for the marketplace of ideas, and inconsistent with the claims about freedom and diversity that most private universities routinely make to students, donors, and others" (Free Speech 101-Volokh, 2017c, para. 21).

It's About Preserving the Right for Speakers to Be Heard

A campus is not compelled to adopt certain speech as its own, but if it doesn't like the message, the college cannot rescind the offer based on the content of the speech, and it must still preserve the right of others to speak. Richard Cohen, president of the Southern Poverty Law Center, drew attention to how many critics of the campus' handling of conservative speakers framed "the issue as a question of whether Milo Yiannopoulos, Richard Spencer, or Ann Coulter have a right to speak on a college campus. In most cases, that is the wrong question" (Free Speech 101-Cohen, 2017d, para. 10). Cohen asserted, "None of those people have any special right to be asked to speak to students" (para. 10). He reframed the issue to understand the proper legal rights of the off-campus speakers by explaining, "But student groups have a right to invite these people to campus, and once they invite them, unless certain rare conditions are met, they have the right to hear what those speakers have to say" (para. 10). In other words, if the college has a policy allowing outside speakers to present on campus, the First Amendment, as applied to public colleges, is interested in protecting the campus community's ability to receive the message if one so chooses to attend the talk. This rule applies "[n]o matter how repugnant one may find a speaker's views, . . . [and the college] cannot pick and choose based on the views the speaker holds" (Free Speech 101-Cohen, 2017d, para. 11).

Campuses Have Speech Interests Too

Campuses have a voice with speech interests and legal rights too. The college is not required to accept, as its own, speakers' messages that counter the college's mission and values. Frederick Lawrence of the Anti-Defamation League, reminded Congress,

> Constitutionally protected hate speech still causes harm to members of our community. There is a moral imperative, therefore, for campus leaders to vigorously criticize hate speech—not to suppress it, not to prohibit it, but to identify it for what it is and criticize it.
> (Challenges to Freedom of Speech I-Lawrence, 2017f, para. 10)

Giving voice to campus leaders, Lawrence reiterated during the question and answer period of the hearing, "University administrators also have First Amendment rights and also get to speak. So in many cases the answer is not to run to the extreme of shutting down an event" (Challenges to Freedom of Speech I-Lawrence, 2017f, para. 28).

Further, during the congressional hearings, interested parties submitted insights and recommendations that would further respect campus free speech. Among them, the Anti-Defamation League Chief Executive Officer, Jonathan Greenblatt, issued a statement, explaining:

> Hate speech is constitutionally protected, but campus administrators also have First Amendment rights—and they should use their bully

pulpit to speak out strongly against such harmful speech. Universities have an obligation to maintain a safe and inclusive environment for all of their students. The most effective responses to hateful speech are those that are timely, specific and direct. Naming the hate sends a strong, supportive message to the community that has been targeted and helps restore a safe and inclusive campus climate.

(Anti-Defamation League, 2017, para. 3)

In short, the messages for this lesson makes clear that offensive, repugnant, and distasteful speech is best countered with additional speech denouncing the opposed speech and reaffirming the institution's mission and values.

All Expressions Are Not Equal

The value of expressions are not equal, and harassing comments and messages conveyed as threats onto another shall not be tolerated. For the most part, private colleges may adopt such language that forbids such expressive conduct. Likewise, public colleges may, consistent with the First and Fourteenth Amendments, construct similar prohibitions into student code of conduct policies. Frederick Lawrence explained, "Many states have some form of assault law that proscribes the creation of fear or terror in a victim. These laws, variously enacted as 'menacing,' 'intimidation,' and 'threatening' statutes, may be violated through the defendant's use of words alone" (Challenges to Freedom of Speech I-Lawrence, 2017f, para. 31). Illustrating prohibited conduct sourced originally through a person's expression, Lawrence advised, "'Intimidation' statutes which criminalize words used to coerce others through fear of serious harm, are constitutional so long as it is clear that they apply only when the words are purposely or knowingly used by the accused to produce fear and that the threat is real" (para. 32). Other language distinctions also make certain prohibited conduct not protected under the First Amendment. Lawrence cited "'menacing' statutes [that] differ from 'intimidation' statutes. Whereas 'intimidation' statutes focus upon coercion, the gravamen of menacing is the specific intent to cause fear" (para. 32). Suffice it to say, words that arise to actionable consequences such as coercion or intention to cause fear of serious harm have fallen outside the boundaries of First Amendment protected free speech.

We Sometimes Fail to Protect Free Speech

As noted above, distancing and denouncing speech is a viable tactic to counter offensive, repugnant, and distasteful messages that are contrary to the college's mission and values. Likewise, respecting permissible speech is critical, yet as the anecdotal events raised among the congressional hearing illustrate, campus leaders fail, at times, to take a stance protecting free speech when the opportunity arises. As Michael Zimmerman, the former provost of the Evergreen State College urged, "College administrators need the courage to do what is right, to stand for principles rather than expediency, and to risk alienating some in the name of those principles. Where such strong leadership exists conflict rarely escalates to crisis" (Challenges to Freedom of Speech I-Zimmerman, 2017d, para. 5).

Similarly, during the first Challenges to Freedom of Speech hearing (2017d), Zimmerman espoused the value of faculty accountability as an equally important action. Zimmerman conveyed,

> At the same time, faculty members need to hold their colleagues accountable. The problems we've seen are not, I am confident, supported by the vast majority of faculty. But most have opted to remain silent, to self-censor. They've ceded control of their institutions to a small but vocal minority.
>
> (para. 6)

Zimmerman rationalized the general silence among the faculty describing,

> This silence is understandable. Speaking out distracts people from their important work in teaching and scholarship while often bringing them into conflict with colleagues. Asking faculty to encourage civil discussion and to celebrate a range of voices and perspectives is asking a great deal, more than we see in our political discourse.
>
> (para. 7)

Likewise, during the question and answer period, Allison Stanger reflected, "What disturbs me about what happened at Middlebury is that I think students were actively encouraged by some members of the faculty to do things that were not in their interest, and that upsets me" (Exploring Free Speech-Stanger, 2017a).

Senator Ted Cruz criticized campus leaders' weak stance on free speech rights, depicting the concerns as administrators "quietly roll over" at the threat of violence. Disappointed about the handling of these free speech issues, he opined that our college campuses are now "[w]here college administrators and faculties have become complicit in functioning essentially as speech police" (Free Speech 101-Cruz, 2017a, para. 2).

Discipline Hecklers and Disruptive Demonstrators

Extending the last lesson, the members of Congress and the witnesses generally conveyed interest in campus leaders exercising more authority, particularly by disciplining hecklers and disruptive demonstrators. Professor Volokh (2017c) offered the most direct observations on this point. He warned, "When universities allow lecturers to be just shouted down—and thus shut down—with impunity, something is very badly wrong in American higher education" (Free Speech 101-Volokh, 2017c, para. 15). Instead, during the question and answer period, he advocated for actions consistent with the violation as he explained, "Behavior that is rewarded is repeated. And when thugs learn that all they need to do to suppress speech is threaten violence, then there will be more such threats" (Free Speech 101-Volokh, 2017c).

Naïve Actions, Unintended Consequences

Adam Carolla, who is best known as a comedian, was perhaps an unusual pick to advise congressional committees on the campus free speech (Challenges to Freedom of Speech I-Carolla, 2017b). Nonetheless, he raised concerns about the coddling of our children, which have some merits. Many college students are at a developmentally different intellectual space than our working adults. Dr. Stanger even remarked how a small minority of Middlebury faculty supporting students' protesting "did not encourage their students to read Charles Murray or listen to him first before drawing their own conclusions about his work or his character, which was their obligation as educators" (Exploring Free Speech-Stanger, 2017a, para. 5). Put simply, campus leaders have an opportunity to educate college students about how seemingly naïve actions may lead to unintended consequences.

Frederick Lawrence also provided great insight about the teaching moment for one student he encountered while serving as university president at Brandeis. He described:

> [Following the] murder of two police officers in "revenge" for the death of Eric Garner and Michael Brown, a prominent student member of the campus Black Lives Matter movement tweeted that she had no sympathy with the police officers. Knowing this student, I believe that what she meant was that she was deeply frustrated and troubled that, in her view, vastly more attention had been paid to the deaths of officers Wenjian Liu and Raphael Ramos in the broader community than was given to the deaths of Garner and Brown. But alas, that is not what she said. And, with "help,"

if that is the right word, from one of the sixty or so students who received the tweet, who posted it on what can best be described as an extremist website, her tweet went viral. As you would imagine, I received enormous pressure from all sides on this set of events. Some urged that the student be thrown out of school or at least lose her financial aid package. Others argued that I should issue a short statement supporting free speech and the right of all members of the community to say what they wished.

(Free Speech 101-Lawrence, 2017f, para. 8)

Yet, as this incident illustrated, there was a tremendous opportunity to educate the student about reactions to events, public conversations, and communication crafting.

CONCLUDING REMARKS

While this chapter was structured to present how the reactive policy making, conformity-driven policy goals, and investigatory and oversight powers are exercised, the discussion in this chapter raises the significance of how legislators at the state and federal levels represent constituents who see religion, particularly Christian beliefs, and political ideology, particularly conservative values, as having not been respected. The Julea Ward Freedom of Conscience Act gained greater attention because of the faculty testimony challenging Ward's religious beliefs rather than simply focusing on the learning components and client interests. Similarly, the Alliance Defending Freedom, which aided in Julea Ward's lawsuit, represents an organization that seeks to correct behaviors that it views as discriminating against religion on college campuses.

Intertwined with the religion and campus treatment, critics continue to assail colleges as bastions of liberalism that unduly advocate for political correctness and limited opportunities to voice opposition, especially in terms of dedicated space on campus such as free speech zones. The Foundation for Individual Rights in Education and Goldwater Institute seek to change the free speech climate, which challenges the now seemingly dominant voices. Yet, as these bills state and the congressional hearings affirm, the critics of higher education free speech practices want campus leaders to take control of their campuses. Their displeasure is much like that of then-California Governor Ronald Reagan, who, in 1967, fired Clark Kerr as president of the University of California System for failing to control the protestors at the Berkeley campus in the 1960s. The difference, however, is that the recently enacted laws and proposed legislation seek thorough investigations and hefty penalties onto the disruptors, demonstrators, and hecklers. Adding more teeth to the consequences of free speech violations, in March 2019, President Trump signed an Executive Order that moves beyond punishing the individuals who violate free speech to punishing campuses by directing federal agencies to ensure that free speech rights are maintained or campuses risk loss of federal dollars (Kreighbaum, 2019; McMurtrie, 2019). The impacts are great, yet if Allison Stanger's experience at Middlebury reflects what many free speech and protest reports show, the free speech intruders are only a "small minority," and as many of the congressional experts testified, the matter is best left to campuses, not lawmakers.

REFERENCES

American Legislative Executive Council (2018). *Forming Open and Robust University Minds (FORUM) Act.* Retrieved from www.alec.org/model-policy/forming-open-and-robust-university-minds-forum-act

Anti-Defamation League (2017, October 26). *ADL to Senate Committee: Hate speech is protected, but harm must be addressed.* Retrieved from www.adl.org/news/press-releases/adl-to-senate-committee-hate-speech-is-protected-but-harm-must-be-addressed

Arizona Amending Sections 13-2906, 15-1861 and 15-1864, Arizona Revised Statutes; Relating to Public Assembly H.B. 2548 (2016).

Arizona Amending Sections 15-1861 and 15-1864, Arizona Revised Statutes; Amending Title 15, Chapter 14, Article 6, Arizona Revised Statutes, By Adding Section 15-1865; Relating to Postsecondary Education, Ariz. H.B. 2615 (2016).

Campus Free Expression Act, Fla. Rev. Stat. § 1004.097 (2019).

Campus Free Expression Act, Mo. Rev. Stat. § 173.1550 (2019).

Campus Free Expression Act, Utah Code § 53B-27–201 (2019).

Campus Free Expression Act, Va. Code Ann. § 23–9.2:13 (2019).

Campus Free Speech Act, Ga. Code § 20-3-48 (2018). (passed in 2018 under SB 339).

Campus Free Speech Protection Act, Ky. Rev. Stat. § 164.348 (2019).

Campus Free Speech Protection Act, Tenn. Code § 49-7-2405 (2017).

Challenges to Freedom of Speech on College Campuses, Part I, Joint Hearing before the House Committee on Oversight and Government Reform, Submission of Healthcare, Benefits, and Administrative Rules and Subcommittee on Intergovernmental Affairs, 115th Cong., 1st Session, Serial No. 115-30 (2017a). (Remarks by Rep. Jim Jordan).

Challenges to Freedom of Speech on College Campuses, Part I, Joint Hearing before the House Committee on Oversight and Government Reform, Submission of Healthcare, Benefits, and Administrative Rules and Subcommittee on

Intergovernmental Affairs, 115th Cong., 1st Session, Serial No. 115-30 (2017b). (Statements of Adam Carolla).

Challenges to Freedom of Speech on College Campuses, Part I, Joint Hearing before the House Committee on Oversight and Government Reform, Submission of Healthcare, Benefits, and Administrative Rules and Subcommittee on Intergovernmental Affairs, 115th Cong., 1st Session, Serial No. 115-30 (2017c). (Statements of Ben Shapiro).

Challenges to Freedom of Speech on College Campuses, Part I, Joint Hearing Before the House Committee on Oversight and Government Reform, Submission of Healthcare, Benefits, and Administrative Rules and Subcommittee on Intergovernmental Affairs, 115th Cong., 1st Session, Serial No. 115-30. (2017d). (Statements of Michael Zimmerman).

Challenges to Freedom of Speech on College Campuses, Part II, Joint Hearing before the House Committee on Oversight and Government Reform, Submission of Healthcare, Benefits, and Administrative Rules and Subcommittee on Intergovernmental Affairs, 115th Cong., 2nd Session, Serial No. 115-105 (2018a). (Statement of Bret Weinstein via www.youtube.com/watch?v= 4YGw9mG_IJg).

Challenges to Freedom of Speech on College Campuses, Part II, Joint Hearing before the House Committee on Oversight and Government Reform, Submission of Healthcare, Benefits, and Administrative Rules and Subcommittee on Intergovernmental Affairs, 115th Cong., 2nd Session, Serial No. 115-105 (2018b). (Statement of Michael Zimmerman).

Christian Legal Society v. Kane, 319 F. App'x. 645 (9th Cir. 2009), cert. granted, No. 08-1371 (U.S. Dec. 7, 2009).

Christian Legal Society v. Martinez, 561 U.S. 661 (2010).

Christian Legal Society v. Walker, 453 F. 3d 853 (7th Cir. 2006).

Derbyshire, J. (2012, April 5). The talk: The nonblack version. *Taki's Magazine.* Retrieved from www.takimag.com/article/the_talk_nonblack_version_ john_derbyshire

Exploring Free Speech on College Campuses Hearing before the Committee on Senate Committee on Health, Education, Labor, and Pensions, 115th Cong., 2nd Session (2017a). (Statement of Allison Stanger).

Forming Open and Robust University Minds (FORUM) Act, Ark. Code § 6-60-1001 et seq. (2019).

Foundation for Individual Rights in Education (2015). *Frequently asked questions: The Campus Free Expression (CAFE) Act.* Philadelphia, PA: FIRE. Retrieved from www.thefire.org/frequently-asked-questions-the-campus-free-expression-cafe-act/

Foundation for Individual Rights in Education (2019). *Spotlight on speech codes, 2019.* Philadelphia, PA: FIRE.

Free Speech 101: The Assault on the First Amendment on College Campuses. Hearing before the Senate Committee on the Judiciary, 115th Cong., 1st Sess. (2017a) (Remarks by Sen. Ted Cruz).

Free Speech 101: The Assault on the First Amendment on College Campuses. Hearing before the Senate Committee on the Judiciary, 115th Cong., 1st Sess. (2017b) (Remarks by Sen. Tim Caine).

Free Speech 101: The Assault on the First Amendment on College Campuses. Hearing before the Senate Committee on the Judiciary, 115th Cong., 1st Sess. (2017c) (Statement of Eugene Volokh).

Free Speech 101: The Assault on the First Amendment on College Campuses. Hearing before the Senate Committee on the Judiciary, 115th Cong., 1st Sess. (2017d) (Statement of J. Richard Cohen).

Free Speech 101: The Assault on the First Amendment on College Campuses. Hearing before the Senate Committee on the Judiciary, 115th Cong., 1st Sess. (2017e) (Statement of Zachary Wood).

Free Speech 101: The Assault on the First Amendment on College Campuses. Hearing Before the Senate Committee on the Judiciary, 115th Cong., 1st Sess. (2017f) (Statement of Frederick Lawrence).

Friedersdorf, C. (2017, August 1). Congress finds consensus on free speech on campus. *The Atlantic*. Retrieved from www.theatlantic.com/politics/archive/2017/08/highlights-from-a-congressional-hearing-on-campus-speech/535515/

Jacobs, J. B. (1993). Implementing hate crime legislation symbolism and crime control. *Annual Survey of American Law 1992/1993*, (4), 541–553.

Jaschik, S. (2018, February 22). Evergreen calls off "Day of Absence." *Inside Higher Ed*. Retrieved from www.insidehighered.com/news/2018/02/22/evergreen-state-cancels-day-absence-set-series-protests-and-controversies

Julea Ward Freedom of Conscience Act: Hearing before the Michigan House Education Committee, Mich. H.B. 5040 (2012a, March 7) (Statement of Judith Kovach, Ph.D.). Retrieved from http://house.michigan.gov/SessionDocs/2011-2012/Testimony/Committee5-3-7-2012-2.pdf

Julea Ward Freedom of Conscience Act: Hearing before the Michigan House Education Committee, Mich. H.B. 5040 (2012b, March 7) (Statement of Michael A. Boulus). Retrieved from http://house.michigan.gov/SessionDocs/2011-2012/Testimony/Committee5-3-7-2012-7.pdf

Julea Ward Freedom of Conscience Act, Mich. S.B. 5040 (2011). Retrieved from www.legislature.mi.gov/documents/2011-2012/billintroduced/Senate/pdf/2011-SIB-0518.pdf

Julea Ward Freedom of Conscience Act, Mich. H.B. 5040 (2012). Retrieved from www.legislature.mi.gov/documents/2011-2012/billengrossed/House/htm/2011-HEBH-5040.htm

Kinery, E. (2017, July 27). Who should police free speech on college campuses? Congress wants to know. *U.S.A. Today*. Retrieved from www.usatoday.com/story/college/2017/07/27/who-should-police-free-speech-on-college-campuses-congress-wants-to-know/37434401/

Kramer, S. (2016, December 20). *When free speech becomes "disorderly conduct": ADF sues GA Gwinnett College*. Scottsdale, AZ: Alliance Defending Freedom. Retrieved from http://adflegal.org/detailspages/blog-details/allianceedge/2016/12/20/when-free-speech-becomes-disorderly-conduct-adf-sues-ga-gwinnett-college

Kreighbaum, A. (2019, Mar. 22). Trump signs broad executive order. *Inside Higher Ed*, https://www.insidehighered.com/news/2019/03/22/white-house-executive-order-prods-colleges-free-speech-program-level-data-and-risk

Kurtz, S., Manley, J., & Butcher, J. (2017). *Campus free speech: A legislative proposal*. Phoenix, AZ: Goldwater Institute.

Larimer, S. (2017, June 20). Senate hearing examines free speech on college campuses after incidents at UC Berkeley and Middlebury. *Washington Post*. Retrieved from www.washingtonpost.com/news/grade-point/2017/06/20/senate-hearing-examines-free-speech-on-college-campuses-after-incidents-at-uc-berkeley-middlebury

Lewis, M. M., Fetter-Harrott, A., Sun, J. C., & Eckes, S. E. (2017). Legal issues related to sexual orientation, gender identity, and public schools. *Social Education*, *81*(5), 315–321.

McMurtrie, B. (2019, Mar. 21). Trump's free-speech order could have been harsher. But higher-ed leaders still don't approve. *Chronicle of Higher Education*. Retrieved from https://www.chronicle.com/article/Trump-s-Free-Speech-Order/245956

Michigan Senate Resolution No. 66, S.R. 66. Retrieved from www.legislature.mi.gov/(S(qwzj1rtycfu54111yfwzsr3i))/mileg.aspx?page=getobject&objectname=2011-SR-0066&query=on

National Association of Social Workers and the Michigan Chapter of the National Association of Social Workers (2011), *Joint Statement National Association of Social Workers and the Michigan Chapter of the National Association of Social Workers in Opposition to S.B. 518 and H.B. 5040*. Retrieved from http://house.michigan.gov/SessionDocs/2011-2012/Testimony/Committee5-3-7-2012-1.pdf

Oppenheimer, M. (2012, Feb. 4). A counselor's convictions put her profession on trial. *New York Times*, A18.

Peters, J. W. (2017, November 22). Using freedom to lead attack on gay rights. *New York Times*, A1.

Peters, J. W. (2018, June 14). In name of free speech, states crack down on campus protests. *New York Times*, A11.

Relating to Universities and Community Colleges, Az. Rev. Stat. 15-1862 (2019).

Restore/Preserve Campus Free Speech Act, N.C. Gen. Stat. § 116-300 (2017). (enacted into law from HB 527 and SB 507 in 2017).

Roll, N. (2017a, September 18). Evergreen professor receives $500,000 settlement. *Inside Higher Ed.* Retrieved from www.insidehighered.com/quicktakes/2017/09/18/evergreen-professor-receives-500000-settlement

Roll, N. (2017b, October 27). Congress rallies around campus free speech. *Inside Higher Ed.* Retrieved from www.insidehighered.com/news/2017/10/27/senate-hearing-explores-free-speech-college-campuses

Saul, S. (2017, May 24). Middlebury disciplines student protesters. *New York Times*, A15.

Stanger, A. (2017, March 13). Understanding the angry mob at Middlebury that gave me a concussion. *New York Times.* Retrieved from www.nytimes.com/2017/03/13/opinion/understanding-the-angry-mob-that-gave-me-a-concussion.html

Students' Right to Speak in a Public Forum, Colo. Rev. Stat. § 23-5-144 (2019).

Svrluga, S. (2016, February 20). Williams College cancels a speaker who was invited to bring in provocative opinions. *Washington Post.* Retrieved from www.washingtonpost.com/news/grade-point/wp/2016/02/20/williams-college-cancels-a-speaker-invited-as-part-of-a-series-designed-to-bring-in-provocative-opinions

Tajfel, H., & Turner, J. (1979). An integrative theory of intergroup conflict. In W. G. Austin & S. Worchel (Eds.), *The social psychology of intergroup relations?* (pp. 33–47). Monterey, CA: Brooks and Cole Publishing Co.

van Klink, B. (2016). Symbolic legislation: An essentially political concept. In B. van Klink, B. van Beers, & L. Poort (Eds.), *Symbolic legislation theory and new developments in biolaw* (pp. 19–35). Cham, Switzerland: Springer International Publishing.

Waldman, A. E. (2012). Tormented: Antigay bullying in schools. *Temple Law Review*, 84(2), 385–442.

Ward v. Polite, 667 F.3d 727 (6th Cir. 2012).

Closing Argument
Challenges, Opportunities, and Strategies

Over 20% of college and university presidents responding to an American Council on Education (ACE) survey perceived the goals of campus inclusion and free speech as being at odds with one another (Espinosa, Crandall, & Wilkinson, 2018). Asked about what that relationship might look like in the future across the nation, 39% said it will worsen, 24% said it will remain the same, 23% anticipated improvement, and 14% were uncertain.

The disheartening outlook of these higher education executives should come as no surprise. Colleges and universities have particular challenges and opportunities when it comes to balancing interests related to free speech and inclusion. They have a unique position in both areas as higher education institutions and face unclear legal terrain with regard to employees and students and free speech. However, and perhaps most importantly, given their role in research and the development and application of knowledge, colleges and universities can play a critically important role in shaping improvements both on campus and in society as a whole (Ben-Porath, 2018).

This work will certainly not be easy. Traditional approaches in higher education to both free speech and inclusion face challenges from both the right and the left (PEN America, 2019), and the variety of roles represented on campus (collectively, within various groups, and even within individuals) bring additional richness and complexity.

> Campus speech controversies have no consistent protagonist or antagonist. University presidents, administrators, faculty, staff, and students can all be cast both in the role of speaker, and that of inhibitor of speech. These permutations vary by controversy, requiring all parties to think carefully about their roles and obligations when it comes to openness, inclusion, and free speech.
>
> (PEN America, 2016, p. 2)

A slight majority of the college presidents responding to the ACE study (Espinosa, Crandall, & Wilkinson, 2018) say they have the tools necessary to address conflicts between free speech and inclusion on their campus. However, it is a very slim majority with 20% saying they do not have the tools and another 29% saying they are not sure.

It is our hope as authors that the preceding chapters have been helpful in easing some of the uncertainty through offering information and analysis of contemporary legal activity and practical suggestions for taking advantage of the unique position higher education holds to fulfill the opportunity afforded to it relative to advancing both free speech (and other First Amendment liberties) and inclusion as important societal values. This concluding chapter builds on the information and suggestions to highlight a series of ideas, which may serve as a broad construct for work on the wide variety of college and university campuses across the United States. We begin with a discussion of the importance of having a broad perspective when gathering information and ideas and a local focus when developing plans and policies. Multiple frameworks that may be used in addressing challenges and opportunities in higher education are then presented. Next we speak to both proactive and reactive measures that might be employed in balancing the interests of free speech and inclusion. The chapter concludes by identifying several principles of practice that can shape our collective efforts.

GLOBAL INFORMATION, LOCAL ACTION

While higher education is uniquely positioned with regard to the challenges and opportunities of balancing free speech and inclusion, it is far from being the only context in which these challenges and opportunities take place. These dynamics play out in settings across our nation and around the world with ideas and information about the theory, practice, and law shaping these developments and being readily available to anyone with an interest in actively seeking them out.

Being well informed about what is taking place elsewhere and giving consideration to the ways in which that knowledge might inform efforts on a particular campus can be a powerful part of the platform upon which policies and practices are developed. This should not be confused, however, with the wholesale adoption of the solution used by someone else from somewhere else. No matter how similar one may perceive them to be or how much one may wish to be like them, to address the situation on your unique campus, a wholesale adoption is ill advised. Higher education is unfortunately prone to the pursuit of so-called *best practices*, particularly when it is confronted with vexing dilemmas. Faced with a variety of constituencies with different interests and a lack of consensus on what the outcomes ought to be or how they should be measured, fields engaged in mimetic isomorphism—they try to look like other organizations in the field that are perceived as successful (Dimaggio & Powell, 1984). Unfortunately too much of what is identified as best practices is often more aptly described as highly publicized practices with absent or inadequate data to support the hype.

We cannot emphasize strongly enough the value in colleges and universities basing their problem-solving and opportunity-building on the unique local characteristics of their institution. Identifying four elements of a campus' environment, the work of Strange and Banning (2015) on campus ecology offers an interesting construct through which higher education institutions can reflect on these characteristics. The *physical environment* includes both the brick-and-mortar elements (or, in the case of online institutions, the network and other computing infrastructure) and the symbolic meaning of places and spaces. Who is present (and who is not), their characteristics, and their relationships and interactions make up the *human aggregate environment*. A third element is the *organization environment*. Strange and Banning describe it as having four features, two of which (degree of formalization and morale) may be particularly important relative to matters of free speech and inclusion. The fourth and final element is the *constructed environment* which is composed of the experiences and perceptions of people about the campus.

Any campus making use of Strange and Banning's (2015) model, or any other model of reflection, about their institution must be mindful of the ways in which minoritized and majority populations may have very different experiences and perceptions reflecting conscious and unconscious bias and systems of privilege and oppression that operate in human systems. Some students, staff, and faculty might find the open quad at the heart of campus with ample shading and plenty of student organization activity as invigorating and welcoming; others may see it as an obstacle course in which they encounter everything from microaggressions to open exclusion or hostility.

IMPORTANCE OF FRAMEWORKS

An important step in advancing a campus-specific approach to policy and practice with regard to free speech and inclusion is actually a step away from the specifics and a step towards building consensus around the broader frameworks for decision-making at the institution. The ways in which we identify, understand, and address a situation are shaped by the conceptual frameworks with which we view our environment. While we have focused much of our attention to this point on legal principles, the law is just one way of considering challenges and opportunities in higher education.

The first, and arguably most important albeit too frequently overlooked of these frameworks, is that of education. Teaching and learning are among the core functions of higher education. There are, of course, many theories of teaching and learning, but the work of Knowles (1984) on andragogy is highlighted here. Whereas *pedagogy* is a more commonly recognized and utilized term, its origins are with the teaching and learning of children. Knowles used the term *andragogy* to describe teaching and learning with adults. Given the demographics of today's students in higher education and the many ways in which they come to campuses with complex and rich life experiences, viewing them as adults rather than children is appropriate. Our reason for centering andragogy, however, goes beyond a focus on these characteristics. We are attracted to the four principles of andragogy articulated by Knowles (1984). They are:

1. Adults ought to be involved in the planning and evaluation of instruction.
2. Experience, including mistakes, serves as the foundation for learning activities.
3. Adults are particularly interested in learning about things that have immediate relevance and impact on their personal lives and work.
4. Rather than being content-driven, adult learning is problem-centered.

How would utilizing andragogy as a framework for addressing free speech (and other First Amendment freedoms) and inclusion look at colleges and universities? Students would be recognized as adults on campus, and their agency would be acknowledged and accepted related to both learning and teaching. What are the things students feel they ought to be learning about in this area? Social media and communication skills? Constructs of social justice? Conflict mediation and advocacy skills? Self-care? Other topics? What might they bring to the conversation in terms of teaching these topics? Life experiences? Cultural capital of resistance and resilience (see the work of Yosso, 2005)? Significant emphasis (not just lip service) would be placed on centering the ways in which individual liberties and collective responsibilities play out in socially just democracies and are connected in important and immediate fashion to the current and future lives of students. What does it mean to be a *socially-just democracy*? What are those liberties and responsibilities? How is it that we have come to our understanding of them, and whose interests are and are not served in the prevailing understanding? Who is responsible for protecting and

146

questioning both? How do affirmation and change come about in society? Finally, ample opportunities would be provided for problem-centered learning with supportive environments for taking risks and making mistakes, both in the curriculum and in the co-curriculum (including a meaningful role in shared governance).

What would the benefits to students and society be of such an approach? There are several. Students could enrich their understanding of their own identities and their sense of what is moral and ethical, which are important goals in the human experience (Patton, Renn, Guido, Quaye, & Evans, 2016; Renn & Reason, 2013). Students might be better prepared to become active participants in our democracy, one of the defining goals of higher education (Hollister, Wilson, & Levine, 2008; Labaree, 1997). Students might also be better prepared to enter the workforce and meet the expectations and needs of employers for workers with critical thinking, problem solving, communication, collaboration, and leadership skills, another of those defining goals (Labaree, 1997; McClellan, Creager, & Savoca, 2018).

In addition to the potential benefits to students and society, higher education institutions might also gain positional advantage in future legal contests related to their policies and practices. Lake (2009) describes the rise of law and legalisms in American higher education in the 1960s to the 1990s, noting that the late 1960s and 1970s were particularly active in this regard. He points to several important ideas that appear in the legal rulings during that time.

> First, and foremost, courts sent the message that the function of higher education was primarily educational. Matters of academic inquiry, for example, were more central to the college mission than, say, athletics or residence life. With the rise of law and legalisms a major first process axiom of higher education law formed: the lowest legal process requirements apply in matters that are purely "academic." The corollary to this axiom was the second axiom of process: matters non-academic or mixed academic/non-academic were to be subject to higher legal process requirements. Outside the classroom, higher education looked a bit like the rest of society. In the classroom, courts appeared especially reticent to interfere with professional academic judgement.
>
> (p. 13)

Sun, Hutchens, and Breslin (2013) have also addressed this topic as it relates to online speech and have offered a curricular nexus test. Taking the work of Lake (2009) and Sun, Hutchens, and Breslin (2013) in conjunction with the strong comments by Justice Stevens in *Christian Legal*

Society v. Martinez (2010), one can begin to imagine a campus which can demonstrate a purposeful and consistent connection between their curricular and co-curricular offerings designed, among other things, to fully engage the campus community in teaching and learning regarding liberties and responsibilities in a socially just democracy as having a compelling affirmative defense if not outright permissible legal ground for their action.

Another powerful framework that has promise is community building. Ernest Boyer, writing about the importance of developing community on college and university campuses, noted six principles of community (Carnegie Foundation for the Advancement of Teaching, 1990). First, campuses should be *educationally purposeful* communities in which faculty and students share academic goals to strengthen teaching and learning. This principle aligns itself well with andragogy as described earlier. *Being just* is the second of the six principles, and it posits an environment in which the sacredness of each person is honored and where diversity is prized and actively pursues. Next, *openness* is described by Boyer as a community which both protects free speech and affirms civility. *Discipline*, the fourth principle, is associated with a community where people accept their responsibilities to the whole and where well-defined governance procedures guide behavior. *Caring* is another of the principles. In a caring community, service to others is encouraged and each member is supported with sensitivity to their unique personhood. The sixth and final principle is being a *celebrative* community in which heritage and in which rituals affirming tradition and change are shared.

The last of the frameworks addressed in this section are Kitchener's (1984) ethical principles. The five principles are: respecting autonomy, being just, benefitting others, doing no harm, and fidelity. *Respecting autonomy* requires that we recognize that individuals should make their own choices congruent with their values. Individuals can benefit from counsel regarding how certain choices may be seen in society and how they may impact on authors. *Doing no harm* obviously includes physical injury, but it also includes other forms of harm as well such as causing emotional hurt or fear or impeding the opportunities of others. *Benefitting others*, a sort of inverse of doing no harm, includes being proactive in lifting others up. It also requires that we help prevent harm to others by stepping forward. Kitchener (1984) is quite clear that *being just* does not mean treating everyone equally but rather "treating equals equally and unequals in unequally but in proportion to their relevant differences" (p. 49)—perhaps troubling language but a notion not inconsistent with concepts of social justice. *Fidelity*, the fifth principle, refers to being loyal and honoring commitments. Put another way, fidelity is marked by one living up to their obligations to others. Developed for use in the practice of professional

148

counseling, the principles are applicable in a variety of human service fields including higher education.

Frameworks may be used in creative and intersecting ways. Imagine what it would be like to learn, work, and live at a college or university where planning, including consideration of the goals of supporting free speech and inclusion, was guided by Knowles's (1984) principles of andragogy, Boyer's principles of community (Carnegie Foundation for the Advancement of Teaching, 1990), and Kitchener's (1984) principles of ethics as informed by contemporary information on the law and communication, particularly a campus where the leaders understand and embrace the idea that there are some things for which it is worth being sued.

Times of challenge relative to free speech and inclusion come and go in the history of our nation. New circumstances and technologies may complicate our discussions in these cycles of disagreement and discord, but we can anchor our ongoing efforts in more timeless frameworks of education, community, ethics, and the law.

PROACTIVE STEPS

Having described the value of maintaining a broad perspective on information, a local focus for action, and a framework for campus decision-making, we turn our attention to a number of proactive measures that colleges and universities may wish to consider as a means of better preparing themselves for those instances in which tensions arise on campus as a result of perceived conflicts between free speech and inclusion. Make no mistake. It is fairly likely that such tensions will occur. The question is how they play out when that happens. Do people on campus store up their grievances because they feel the campus will not hear them or care about them until, after reaching a point of alienation and frustration, they boil over, or do people feel comfortable giving voice to their concerns as they develop given that the campus culture is one of responding with thoughtful care when someone speaks up? Do people feel compelled to create disruptive vehicles for expression, or do they see that there are viable channels for pressing their viewpoints which do not necessitate disruption?

When identifying what they see as effective practices for dealing with these tensions, college and university presidents note a number of proactive steps to help campuses navigate matters of free speech and inclusion (Espinosa, Crandall, & Wilkinson, 2018). We agree with a number of the practices identified by the presidents and amplify on those as well as add a few suggestions of our own in the remainder of this section.

Who is likely to be involved in developing the policies, programs, or responses related to supporting both the values of free speech and inclusion, whether proactive or reactive? While more narrowly focused than

149

a study on the broad spectrum of First Amendment freedoms, a survey of campus presidents about who they count on in addressing conflicts between campus inclusion and free speech values shows that nearly 90% of presidents look to their senior student affairs officer and senior academic officer with 80% looking to legal counsel (Espinosa, Crandall, & Wilkinson, 2018). Note that students and faculty are absent from these responses. While this may reflect a flaw in the design of the study, our sense is that it is a fairly accurate reflection of the perspectives of campus executives. Neoliberal managerialism, which is premised on notions of expertise which reflect systemic biases reflecting embedded privilege and oppression, is an unlikely vehicle for successfully planning for a campus which is both inclusive and a center of free speech. The first of our recommendations for proactive action is for campuses to recognize that the most promising local approaches are those which draw on the collective experiences, insights, and perspectives of all members of the campus community.

Our second proactive recommendation is significantly related to the first. A campus with an environment characterized by a broad, genuine, and respectful relationship and a culture of listening first is better positioned to help assure that a full array of community members feels connected and engaged in its success, including through providing critique and staying involved in working through difficult questions. It is one thing to be angry or frustrated by something about which you care and in which you believe you have a stake; it is entirely another when the object of your anger and frustration is somehow other or outside you.

Our third recommendation for proactive action is to be proactive and inclusive in articulating or revisiting statements of your institution's principles related to First Amendment freedoms. It can be tempting for any number of reasons to seek comfort in pre-packaged, politically popular best-practices boilerplates (see the discussion earlier in this chapter) such as what is commonly referred to as the Chicago Principles (Stone, Bertrand, Olinto, Siegler, Strauss, Warren, & Woodward, 2014) or the *PEN America Principles on Campus Free Speech* (PEN America, 2016). The most promising pathways to principles which will balance the values held by colleges and universities with regard to both inclusion and support for First Amendment freedoms are those which reflect the local institutional context, history, traditions, culture, and populations (Ben-Porath, 2018).

Whether it is describing broad principles and values or articulating specific policies and practices, the fourth proactive recommendation is to be clear about what it is your college or university intends to do and then be consistent in doing that. Put more simply, and echoing an often stated truism of legal advice and professional practice, say what you will do and then do what you say.

An additional recommendation relates to developing knowledge and skills in students, staff, and faculty that can proactively strengthen those individuals and the campus community collectively in ways that help lead to more meaningful discourse on individual freedoms and inclusion. Such opportunities should include both curricular and co-curricular offerings for students and professional development for staff and faculty.

Michigan State University's College of Law made use of a gift from donor Richard McLellan to create the McLellan Online Free Speech Library, a web-based resource for high school students offering the practical information on free speech questions related to social media Ward and Costello (2019). The resource presents the information in ways that are particularly relevant to students' lives. How much of a song can they post? Can they be disciplined for comments made online about a faculty member? This is an interesting idea that could be adapted for use in higher education settings to serve students, staff, and faculty.

There can be value in offering training to staff and faculty on how to handle protests, including disruptions. Be sure to share how individuals may be helpful and where the limits of their authority and responsibility reside. Also, share how the campus will deal with disruption. Implicit in this is the assumption that the campus has developed a general plan for such matters. If not, it could be a good investment of time to do so. There may be differing opinions on who should be playing certain roles or making specific determinations. For example, who will announce to protestors that their action constitutes to disruption and will be dealt with accordingly if it does not come to a rapid conclusion? Who will make the decision as to whether or not to arrest a student, staff, or faculty member involved in a protest?

Do not limit efforts only to offerings on campus. Encourage members of the campus community to read widely and share what they are reading for discussion. Support students, staff, and faculty in attending learning opportunities off campus, whether drive-in or multiple day conferences or computer-mediated presentations. Particularly encourage participation in learning experiences that encourage a move beyond passive learning to actively being involved in problem-based exercises. One wonders how much progress we might make in this area if we spent more time in helping people learn how to have difficult conversations, advocate for change, and serve as an ally than we do in helping them learn how to fill out forms, file reports, or provide depositions or testimony.

Speaking of legal proceedings, here is a sixth recommendation. Do not wait until there is a problem to consult counsel. Regular conversations with a representative of your college's or university's legal team about what has been going on around campus and what might be coming up is time well spent. Develop a relationship of openness and trust, and a mutual understanding of one another's roles and perspectives related to issues of free speech and inclusion.

Our seventh and final recommendation related to proactive measures has to do with event planning, whether curricular or co-curricular. It can help to keep in mind that the situations which have become significant on campuses occupy a great deal of attention in various forms of media. That is understandable, and it may be instructive in that those stories provide the impetus for revisiting our assumptions, practices, and policies. However, it is helpful to keep in mind that those situations are a modest slice of all the events on college and university campuses across this nation in any given year. Lots of speakers, programs, presentations, and protests occur in ways that offer evidence that it is possible for higher education institutions to support both free speech and inclusion. Learning from when it goes well can be as powerful as learning from when it goes less well, and we ought not be in the business of crafting our policies and practices around worst case scenarios as doing so can be in contradiction to both our espoused values and our core mission.

REACTIVE STEPS

What steps might colleges and universities take when issues of free speech and inclusion come front and center on their campus? We offer several recommendations for reactive steps in this section of the chapter.

We begin here as we did with our discussion of possible proactive steps. About 90% of college presidents report that they look to senior student affairs officers to play an important role when an active conflict is taking place on their campus related to First Amendment freedoms and inclusion (Espinosa, Crandall, & Wilkinson, 2018). A full 80% identify the chief communications officer and chief of campus police as playing a similarly important role. It is striking to us that academic leadership (including faculty) and student leadership are not seen in the same way. One has to wonder why this is the case? Do presidents see these administrative leaders as being particularly well prepared? Does it reflect that presidents feel pressure to find an administrative decision for which they can command an answer quickly as opposed to a consensus-driven response that might require more time to reveal itself? Our first recommendation is that presidents quickly take stock of their assumptions about the nature of the situation before them and consider the ways in which those assumptions are shaping responses. What is the nature of what is being presented? Is this perceived as a normative part of campus life, or is it seen as an aberration? What are the goals? Is the solution to get to quiet? Media management?

Learning? What, if any, are the real deadlines and hard limits related to moving forward? Is there a sense of urgency? If so, what drives it? Will the institution engage in a give and take, or will it insist on a set of conditions before engaging in addressing grievances? Making the most of the opportunities afforded to an institution when free speech and inclusion are seemingly at cross purposes is unlikely if the situation is seen as a problem or a crisis which must be resolved. Rather, a focus on coming to a shared understanding which provides a platform upon which a better future can be built may offer greater promise.

A related recommendation and one which we identify as being co-first is for campus leadership, including students, staff, and faculty, to breathe! The matter at hand is important and requires clarity of thinking, communication, and action. Grasping for the first thing that makes things feel better may offer temporary relief but serve as a distraction from long-term substantive solutions. As one of the co-authors frequently shared with colleagues, we may not control the agenda but almost always control the clock. Give the campus the gift of time to work through the feelings, frustrations, and future opportunities together.

Community forums or meetings between university officials and leaders of the affected groups are common steps at colleges and universities at times such as these, but how often have you heard about these interactions going wrong? A second recommendation is to prioritize listening over speaking. There is likely a strong need for a statement of recognition and affirmation of values (discussed next), but there is almost certainly an equally pressing need to hear from all involved about their feelings and observations. These expressions may be difficult to hear, but it is very important that they be heard. It can be tempting to offer explanations or somehow 'correct' the record. In the colloquial expression of our time, not today Satan! Listen with empathy and without judgment. There may be a point in the process where coming to some common understanding of what has transpired will be a necessary component of developing a plan for moving forward, but that point is unlikely to be successfully reached without first allowing folks to give voice to their immediate and visceral response.

We offered a co-first recommendation, and here we offer a co-second. A clear, concise, and unambiguous statement of the college or university's position needs to be shared fairly early in response to any situation in which there is significant tension centering around inclusion and free speech. There may be a tendency to wait until all the facts are in before taking a position or to give something to all sides in the statement. Those are strategies fraught with problems. A determination of 'the facts' may never be forthcoming as situations such as these can result from competing interpretations of facts upon which all parties agree or on widely varying understanding of fact based on perspective. Further, constructing what is taking place as a contest between sides can further exacerbate the situation and make moving forward together more problematic. It is likely that all parties involved will say with sincerity that they value both free speech and inclusion; they just construct the practice of those two ideals differently given the current context. The institutional statement should acknowledge the validity of the concerns and feelings being expressed, affirm the commonality of values, and avoid essentializing law or policy as the sole basis upon which the institution will move forward. Support for the mission and for the people of the campus ought to be at the heart of the statement, recognizing that this support is informed by a variety of factors. All of the other factors can be discussed, if necessary, in subsequent statements. The first institutional statement should be about people and values.

Another recommendation is to tend to the safety and well-being of all members of the campus community if the situation at hand is one which leaves students, staff, or faculty feeling threatened or disenfranchised. This requires sensitivity to sociohistorical circumstances which, if not given consideration, might lead to a failure to recognize or appreciate the differing ways in which some speech may be perceived. The test here is not whether the powerful or privileged feel safe or have a sense of well-being.

Two additional recommendations hearken back to advice offered in the preceding section. One is, having articulated policies and practices related to these matters, act in ways consistent with them. Having said what you will do, do what you said. Doing otherwise invites the observation that institutional responses reflect biases of one type or another or are based upon content-driven considerations. The other is, while it is prudent to seek the advice of counsel, keep in mind that it is just that—advice. That information is one part of a decision-making framework, and it should be given appropriate credence and respect. The situation may be such that legal advice in the matter is a compelling reason for a particular choice. It may also be the case that it shapes a choice but does not define it.

CONCLUSION

We have cited the perceptions of college presidents throughout this chapter, and we begin our closing comments in the same spirit. While clearly recognizing the contemporary challenges in supporting free speech and inclusion on college campuses, higher education executives appear at least somewhat sanguine about the future of these matters on their campuses. Nearly a third see the relationship between these values as improving in the future, and nearly half see it as remaining about the same (Espinosa, Crandall, &

Wilkinson, 2018). Only 9% believe it will worsen and another 10% are uncertain. It is our belief that there is reason to be hopeful because there appears to be a collective will among students, staff, and faculty to provide leadership in creating a better relationship.

The authors of this book concur with the assertion that efforts to ensure openness and inclusion need not be in conflict with efforts to protect and promote First Amendment freedoms (PEN America, 2017). Rather, both notions are essential imperatives for the robust future of higher education and our nation. We are mindful, however, that for many students, particularly students from minoritized groups, the essential tension is not between speech and inclusion but simply, clearly, personally, and powerfully about campus climate, safety, and inclusion. "Indeed, hiding behind the First Amendment in response to students' deeper demands to reckon with growing hate, intimidation, and racism risks alienating a rising generation of activists, leaders, and scholars from the fundamental tenets of free expression" (PEN America, 2019, p. 27).

We find ourselves drawn to Ben-Porath's (2018) idea of inclusive freedom as a pathway forward.

> This approach takes seriously the importance of a free and open exchange as a necessary condition for the pursuit of knowledge and as a contributing condition to the development of civic and democratic capacities,—that's the "freedom" part—while lending similar weight to the related demand that all members of the campus community be able to participate in this free and open exchange if it is to accomplish the goals of free inquiry, open-minded research, and equal access to learning and to civic development—that's the "inclusive" part.
>
> (p. 2)

In closing, we are reminded of the words of Dr. Martin Luther King, Jr. "The arc of the moral universe is long, but it bends toward justice." As Mychal Denzel Smith (2018) points out, however, these words paraphrase a more complicated but very relevant message from Theodore Parker, an abolitionist. Rev. Parker, during a sermon in 1853, observed,

> I do not pretend to understand the moral universe. The arc is a long one. My eye reaches but little ways. I cannot calculate the curve and complete the figure by experience of sight. I can divine it by conscience. And from what I see I am sure it bends toward justice.
>
> (as cited in Smith, 2018, p. 5)

Smith points out the difference between King's simpler phrasing and Parker's original comments is that the former asserts inevitability while the latter implies some uncertainly. Smith goes on to note that assuring that the arc does indeed draw upward is a function of both definition and effort. We must begin with a shared sense of the nature of the challenge and opportunity and an idea of where it is that we wish to go. We can then collectively go about the business of getting there. If nothing else, we hope this book has served as a call for higher education to do just that with regard to supporting both First Amendment freedoms and inclusion at colleges and universities across our nation.

REFERENCES

Ben-Porath, S. (2018, October 12). *"LOL I will never be fired": Campus free speech in the era of social media.* Retrieved from www.law.berkeley.edu/wp-content/uploads/2018/10/LOL-I-will-never-be-fired.pdf

Carnegie Foundation for the Advancement of Teaching (1990). *Campus life: In search of community.* Princeton, NJ: Author.

Christian Legal Society v. Martinez, 561 U.S. 661 (2010).

Dimaggio, P. J., & Powell, W. W. (1984). The iron cage revisited: Institutional isomorphism and collective rationality in organizational fields. *American Sociological Review, 48*(2), 147–160.

Espinosa, L. L., Crandall, J. R., & Wilkinson, P. (2018, April 9). *Free speech and campus inclusion: A survey of college presidents.* Washington, DC: American Council on Education. Retrieved from www.higheredtoday.org/2018/04/09/free-speech-campus-inclusion-survey-college-presidents/

Hollister, R. M., Wilson, N., & Levine, P. (2008). Educating students to foster active citizenship. *Peer Review, 10*(2/3). Retrieved from www.aacu.org/publications-research/periodicals/educating-students-foster-active-citizenship

Kitchener, K. S. (1984). Intuition, critical evaluation and ethical principles: The foundation for ethical decisions in counseling psychology. *Counseling Psychologist, 12*(43), 43–55.

Knowles, M. S. (1984). *The adult learner: A neglected species* (3rd ed.). Houston, TX: Gulf Publishing.

Labaree, D. F. (1997). Public goods, private goods: The struggle over educational goals. *American Educational Research Journal, 34*(1), 39–81.

Lake, P. (2009). *Beyond discipline: Managing the modern higher education environment.* Bradenton, FL: Hierophant Enterprises.

McClellan, G. S., Creager, K., & Savoca, M. (2018). *A good job: Campus employment as a high-impact practice.* Sterling, VA: Stylus.

Patton, L. D., Renn, K. A., Guido, F. M., Quaye, S. J., & Evans, N. J. (2016) *Student development in college: Theory, research, and practice* (3rd ed.). San Francisco: Jossey-Bass

PEN America (2016). *PEN America principles on campus free speech.* New York: Author. Retrieved from https://pen.org/sites/default/files/PEN%20America%20Principles%20on%20Campus%20Free%20Speech.pdf

PEN America (2017, June 15). *And campus for all: Diversity, inclusion, and freedom of speech at U.S. universities.* New York: Author. Retrieved from https://pen.org/wp-content/uploads/2017/06/PEN_campus_report_06.15.2017.pdf

PEN America (2019, April 2). *Chasm in the classroom: Campus free speech in a divided America.* New York: Author. Retrieved from https://pen.org/wp-content/uploads/2019/04/2019-PEN-Chasm-in-the-Classroom-v3.pdf

Renn, K. A., & Reason, R. D. (2013). *College students in the United States: Characteristics, experiences, and outcomes.* San Francisco: Jossey-Bass.

Smith, M. D. (2018, January 18). The truth about "the arc of the moral universe." *Huffington Post.* Retrieved from www.huffpost.com/entry/opinion-smith-obama-king_n_5a5903e0e4b04f3c55a252a4

Stone, G. R., Bertrand, M., Olinto, A., Siegler, M., Strauss, D. A., Warren, K. W., & Woodward, A. (2014). *Report on the committee on freedom of expression.* University of Chicago. Retrieved from https://provost.uchicago.edu/sites/default/files/documents/reports/FOECommitteeReport.pdf

Strange, C. C., & Banning, J. H. (2015). *Educating by design: Creating colleges and universities that work.* San Francisco: Jossey-Bass.

Sun, J. C., Hutchens, N. H., & Breslin, J. D. (2013). A (virtual) land of confusion with college students' online speech: Introducing the curricular nexus test. *University of Pennsylvania Journal of Constitutional Law, 16*(1), 49–96.

Ward, K., & Costello, N. (2019, March 1). Students + social media + free speech = A volatile mix. *MSU Today.* Retrieved from https://msutoday.msu.edu/news/2019/students-social-media-free-speech-a-volatile-mix/

Yosso, T. J. (2005). Whose culture has capital? A critical race theory discussion of community cultural wealth. *Race, Ethnicity, and Education, 8*(1), 69–91.

Index

Note: Page numbers in **bold** indicate tables; page numbers that include n indicate notes.

165

recommendations: digital
communications 104–107;
free speech protections 81–83;
proactive 150–152; reactive
152–154
"redeeming value," and free speech 6
"Redefining the Obligation to
Protect Students" (article) [Jaschik]
101, 131
Regents of the University of
California v. Bakke 17
Regents of the University of
Michigan v. Ewing 32
Registered (or Recognized) Student
Organizations (RSOs) 78–80; and
limited public forums 69
"Regulating Hate Speech and the
First Amendment: The Attractions
of, and Objections to, an Explicit
Harms-Based Analysis" (article)
[Turner] 14
Relating to Universities and
Community Colleges, Az. Rev.
Stat. 15–1862 (2019) 118
religion: freedom of 79; liberty bills
and LGBTQ equity 118; see also
court cases; U.S. Supreme Court
Religious Liberty and Conscience
Protection Act, Julea Ward
Freedom of Conscience Act 118;
see also Ward v. Polite
Renn, K. A., and Reason, R. D.,
College Students in the
United States: Characteristics,
Experiences, and Outcomes
(book) 147
Report on the Committee on
Freedom of Expression (report)
[Stone, Bertrand, Olinto, Siegler,
Strauss, Warren, and Woodward]
83, 89, 150, 157; see also Chicago
principles
Resnick, G., and Collins, B., "Milo
Yiannopoulos Is Getting Paid Big,

So Will He Give away the Money
He Promised?" 1
"Resolution of EMU Case
Confirms ACA Code Of Ethics:
Counseling Profession's Stance
against Client Discrimination"
(article) [Rudow] 47
Responding to Campus Protests:
A Practitioner Resource (book)
[Sun, Hutchens, and Sponsler] 3, 5,
10–11, 21
Responses to Importance of
Democratic Values on Campus 20
Restore/Preserve Campus Free
Speech Act, N.C. Gen. Stat.
§ 116-300 (2017) 121, 142
Reyns, B. W., Henson, B., and Fisher,
B. S., "Deviance: Low Self-Control
and Opportunity as Explanations
of Sexting among College
Students" 102 (article); see also
sexting
Rhoads, R. A.: Freedom's Web:
Student Activism in an Age of
Cultural Diversity (book) 28;
"Student Activism, Diversity, and
the Struggle for a Just Society"
(article) 12
rights, clashing 1, 3
"right to be forgotten," and erasure
of personal data 95; see also
privacy
"Right to be forgotten" [Intersoft
consulting] 95
"Right to Be Racist in College, The:
Racist Speech, White Institutional
Space, and the First Amendment"
(article) [Moore and Bell] 27
Rise Above Movement 18
Robinson, C., "Haley Barber
Apologizes for Racist Video, Says
She Was Expelled from University
Of Alabama" (article) 101–102
Rock for Life-UMBC v. Hrabowski 75

175